P9-CFY-962

DESIGNING worship

creating and integrating
powerful God experiences

kim miller

Group

Loveland, Colorado

www.grouppublishing.com

Group resources actually work!

This Group resource helps you focus on **"The 1 Thing"**—a life-changing relationship with Jesus Christ. "The 1 Thing" incorporates our **R.E.A.L.** approach to ministry. It reinforces a growing friendship with Jesus, encourages long-term learning, and results in life transformation, because it's:

Relational
Learner-to-learner interaction enhances learning and builds Christian friendships.

Experiential
What learners experience through discussion and action sticks with them up to 9 times longer than what they simply hear or read.

Applicable
The aim of Christian education is to equip learners to be both hearers and doers of God's Word.

Learner-based
Learners understand and retain more when the learning process takes into consideration how they learn best.

Designing Worship
Creating and Integrating Powerful God Experiences

All weekend worship sermons referred to in this book are available online at www.ginghamsburg.org in their complete form in print and in streaming video.

Credits

Chief Creative Officer: Joani Schultz
Editor: Jennifer Wilger
Copy Editor: Loma Huh
Book Designer: Jean Bruns
Print Production Artist: Pat Miller

Cover Designer: Sarah Gillenwater
Production Manager: Peggy Naylor
All interior illustration and photography © Ginghamsburg Church and used by permission. Special thanks to Brent Thurston.

Unless otherwise noted, Scripture taken from the HOLY BIBLE, NEW INTERNATIONAL VERSION®. Copyright © 1973, 1978, 1984 by International Bible Society. Used by permission of Zondervan Publishing House. All rights reserved.

Library of Congress Cataloging-in-Publication Data
Miller, Kim, 1956–
   Designing worship : creating and integrating powerful God experiences / Kim Miller.-- 1st American pbk. ed.
       p. cm.
   ISBN 0-7644-2681-8 (pbk. : alk. paper)
   1. Worship. I. Title.
   BV10.3.M55 2004
   264--dc22
                                                 20040021
22

10 9 8 7 6 5 4 3 2 1   13 12 11 10 09 08 07 06 05 04

Printed in the United States of America.

contents

17 39 *

109933

When Jesus left the planet Earth, he empowered a team to carry on the movement of God. At Ginghamsburg Church, we call this mission strategy "the priesthood of all believers"—ordinary people radically serving through the love and power of an extraordinary God. The biblical picture of this is the body of Christ—servants joining forces to carry out what one person cannot execute alone.

The downside of the large churches of the '90s is that they were susceptible to the cult of personality. What will happen when the leaders of the megachurch movement are gone? The church of the future must rediscover its ancient roots and be led forward by teams rather than by just star performers. The postmodern church must practice the priesthood of all believers as we engage and launch Jesus followers into authentic ministry through their own call and giftedness.

For the last decade, Kim Miller has practiced team leadership in worship arts and in our senior management team at Ginghamsburg Church. She has effectively integrated worship into our congregational life as a whole.

This book presents powerful insights and creative ideas from Kim's years of building and working through teams.

Mike Slaughter
Lead Pastor, Ginghamsburg Church

I've always had worship dreams. I began attending church in sixth grade at the invitation of my older sister. Even while sitting in worship at that age, I could never keep myself from dreaming about how it *could* be. Ways we could *do it better.* Songs that would *say it better.* Dramas that could *illustrate* the point using real situations from everyday life. Ideas for *connecting* people more effectively.

I've been living these dreams as a part of the worship design team here at Ginghamsburg, a United Methodist church in Tipp City, Ohio, since 1995. I was experienced in drama and fairly good at recruiting. (I solicited the services of my family and friends, assuring them they would be great on stage!) These skills would serve me well for my initial assignment: to write a drama for the first Welcome Weekend in our then-new building.

The majority of my work on the team in those early days was writing dramas based on popular culture. *The Brady Bunch* became "The Broody Bunch Goes to Church." *Live! with Regis & Kathie Lee* became "Travis & Chatty Lee with Morning Latte." I loved the work and discovered that I was totally energized by reaching Ginghamsburg's target audience—people turned off or out by traditional church.

I was good at writing dramas. What I wasn't good at was staying home on worship design team day. I had this bad habit of coming back...even though I was unpaid for my first few years on the team. I was told not to think of it as a "real job," for it would never be a paying gig. Once, after coming home from a long vacation, I was told I could certainly still have this "job" because no one else had asked for it or wanted it!

After sticking around for a long time, I finally got a small cubby of my own. When I just wouldn't go away, my persistence paid off. I got "promoted" to half time, then full time, and eventually named as team leader. I highly recommend the persistence method as a way of starting a creative career. It keeps you humble and makes a great story. Even Steven Spielberg required persistence to jump-start his career. In his early years in Hollywood, he set up his own rickety desk in a corner of Universal Studios and just pretended he was employed there. He worked hard at whatever he could find to do, until one day the folks at Universal decided he just *had* to stay.

Like Spielberg and others, I just *have* to stay. Day after day, the desire to connect people to God through worship draws me back. At Ginghamsburg, we refer to these worship connections as "God experiences." God experiences vary in nature, but people must have them in order to know love and hope, direction and meaning for life. Adam and Eve encountered God after eating the forbidden fruit (Genesis 3). Abraham heard a word from God just as the ax was to come down on his son, Isaac (Genesis 22). Moses experienced God calling to him from a flaming bush (Exodus 3–4). David had a heart-wrenching God experience as he repented of his own deep sin (Psalm 51).

I want to believe that it is possible for post-modern pilgrims to have powerful God experiences as well. While worship designers cannot *make* that happen in the context of our weekly worship celebrations, we can certainly *prepare* the place where God can powerfully show up. Through the use of video, music, and graphic and visual arts, we can create an environment that stimulates all the senses to focus on God in worship. Then we can step back and allow the Holy Spirit to move—to do God's best work in the lives of real people. That's my dream. And in my wildest imaginings I never thought I'd some-day have a real job that allows me to participate in realizing this dream. But I do—and perhaps you do, too!

> I want to believe that it is possible for postmodern pilgrims to have powerful God experiences as well. While worship designers cannot *make* that happen in the context of our weekly worship celebrations, we can certainly *prepare* the place where God can powerfully show up.

My mission statement as a worship designer is "to connect people to Jesus in creative ways," and I've always believed that I can best do that within the context of weekly worship. It's been my experience that the weekly worship celebration is

- the best place for fallen people to encounter a redeemer God,
- the best environment for community connection,
- the best format to set new direction for a faith movement,
- the best atmosphere to review core values of a faith community, and
- the best opportunity to introduce lost sheep to the loving Shepherd.

Luke's Gospel describes the relationship between lost sheep and Jesus, the Good Shepherd, this way:

"Suppose one of you has a hundred sheep and loses one of them. Does he not leave the ninety-nine in the open country and go after the lost sheep until he finds it?" (Luke 15:4)

At Ginghamsburg, we don't worry too much about the ninety-nine sheep. Like Jesus, our good shepherd, we are in it for the one. I love the challenge of dreaming up new ways to search for sheep in postmodern culture. As we design our worship, we strive to create wonderful and imaginative worship experiences that will entice the one lost sheep back into the fold.

And in my wildest dreams, it *will* happen! Connecting broken people to an experience of God is not a mission for those who seek a comfortable life or a predictable vocation. Designing powerful worship events for postmodern people is crazy. It's messy; it's inconvenient; it's costly. But when the one lost sheep comes skipping back into the pen, it all seems worth it.

What are *your* wildest dreams? And in those wild dreams are you effectively connecting ordinary people to an extraordinary God? Is it your dream to create powerful God experiences?

As you read this book and view the accompanying DVD, I hope a glimpse into my wild dreams will help you

• assemble and empower your own dynamic worship team,

• find strength to persevere in challenging times of ministry,

• integrate music, media, and message in your weekly worship celebrations, and

• rekindle your own passion for creating powerful God experiences.

Now, let's start dreaming…

developing…

and designing worship!

1. Behind the Scenes With the Ginghamsburg Worship Team. Watch members of the Ginghamsburg worship team dream, develop, and deploy a weekend worship celebration. Narrated by Kim Miller.
- View in conjunction with Chapters 5 and 6
- Time: 5:43

2. Resurrection Mike. Meet Mike Martindale, a beloved Jesus follower from the Ginghamsburg congregation. When he was sixteen, Mike fell off a three-wheeler and slipped into a coma for three months. As you listen to Mike's story, you'll be reminded of God's power and hope in the lives of everyday people.
- Topic: Resurrection
- Scripture: Acts 2
- Desired Outcome: to move forward in the power of the Resurrection
- Time: 5:00

3. I Have a Dream? As serious kingdom builders, we must ask ourselves if Dr. Martin Luther King Jr.'s dream is any closer to reality than when he was alive. Is our nation truly uniting? Does it truly celebrate its unique and diverse population? What is the church's role in this process? These on-the-street interviews take an honest look at these questions as they explore average people's responses to this ongoing challenge. A great piece to use during the observation of Martin Luther King Jr.'s birthday.
- Topic: Racism
- Scripture: Ephesians 2:14-16
- Desired Outcome: to become genuinely committed to the pursuit of racial harmony
- Time: 1:30

4. Socks Knocks. Discover what Jesus has in common with a stray cat by learning about Socks, the cat who just wanted to live inside his owner's house.
- Topic: Fear of commitment
- Scripture: Revelation 3:20
- Desired Outcome: to totally surrender our lives to Jesus
- Time: 2:58

5. Life's Moments. A series of natural, human, and urban images, this piece was originally edited without a music bed of its own to accompany the featured song, "Great Light of the World," by Bebo Norman, but it could easily be used as a backdrop for a song of your own choosing.
- Time: 5:27

6. What Is Your Wildest Life Dream? This series of on-the-street interviews challenges viewers to scrutinize their own lives and the purposes for which they were created.
- Topic: Aspirations
- Scripture: Luke 24:32; Hebrews 11:1-2
- Desired Outcome: to move past fear and pursue God's purposes
- Time: 3:55

As you begin the process of designing worship, you may be humbled by the enormity of the task. What if no one is willing to help? What if your budget doesn't match up with your dreams? What if your first worship event fails to inspire?

I'm here to tell you, "That's OK!" As worship designers, we must give ourselves permission to make mistakes—especially in the beginning. Writers call it the "rough draft"; in worship design, I call it "pretending" or "dreaming." Each time we begin work on a worship event at Ginghamsburg, we say, "Chances are slim that we'll get this right the first time, so let's just focus on what we can see at this point and give ourselves permission to change and improve it later on."

PART ONE: Getting Started

"The first cut is the deepest."
ROD STEWART

As the team leader, it's your job to create an atmosphere of permission and possibility within which your team can work. Any creative project, large or small, will be best developed in this type of atmosphere, and worship design is no exception. As you brainstorm with your team, you'll find yourself discarding as many ideas as you keep. Initially, it may be hard to reach consensus. But as your team works together over time, and as you entrust your mission to God's leading, your collective creativity will eventually breathe life into the worship events you dream together.

Whether you're designing a powerful worship experience, writing a book, or cleaning out the garage, getting started is half the job. In the following chapters, you'll find a road map to help you get started, including direction for
- finding team members for your worship design team,
- developing job descriptions to define your team,
- forging a strong connection with your lead pastor or speaker, and
- empowering your team to create powerful God experiences for any size church.

While the task may seem overwhelming at first, if we can force ourselves to go beyond *thinking* about it and begin *doing* it, we'll be on our way. So let's do it!

CHAPTER 1

Assembling a Worship Design Team

"In the middle of difficulty lies opportunity."

ALBERT EINSTEIN

H ow did we start designing worship as a team at Ginghamsburg? We started in the middle of great difficulty, as I'll describe in the following pages. Through a series of perspective-shifting events, the opportunity arose to pull together a worship design team. But before there was the worship design team, there was the worship. Worship is critical to what we do here at Ginghamsburg. Our mission statement is "*Bring* seeking people into a life-Celebration of Jesus. *Grow* as disciples in Cell community. *Serve* out of our Call and giftedness." Powerful worship celebrations are essential to *bring seeking people* into the church. But what is a "powerful worship celebration"?

> "*Bring* seeking people into a life-Celebration of Jesus. *Grow* as disciples in Cell community. *Serve* out of our Call and giftedness."

The multisensory worship style we embrace at Ginghamsburg evolved in response to a "light-bulb moment." Our pastor, Mike Slaughter, had seen a speaker do a presentation augmented by computer-generated slides. Mike was struck by the potential of that technology, and a mental light bulb came on as he realized that pictures and visual images could be a powerful way to communicate the greatest story ever told. For the church to remain effective into the future, Mike concluded, we must cease telling the story through "talking heads" alone and begin to incorporate multimedia into our worship. Mike dreamed of worship services where storytelling and artistic imagery would invite worshippers to participate in the process, using their senses and powerful mental capabilities to encounter God more deeply.[1]

Armed with this vision, in 1995 Ginghamsburg moved into a new worship facility that was media-capable. But despite the media-friendly new church building, challenges arose. No one on staff knew much about the equipment. The music director had never considered what connection the music might have with visual imagery, and simply showing random pictures during a worship celebration does not effective storytelling make. Thus a primitive version of the worship design team was formed, in the belief that what no one person could pull off alone, many people together might actually have a shot at.

When it comes to designing worship, teamwork is absolutely essential. If we still think we can plan the most precious hour of the week in a vacuum, shame on us! Even as worship designers, how can we think we have all the best ideas about appropriate music, drama, sermon themes, or visual imagery? When we do have good ideas of our own, we're tempted to claim solo credit by saying, "God gives those pieces to me." Maybe so, but remember that even God is a team of three parts.

> "Let *us* make man in *our* image"
> (Genesis 1:26).

A LEADER WORTH FOLLOWING

During Jesus' ministry on earth, he assembled and led a team of twelve. Twelve ordinary people with sometimes conflicting, sometimes complementary ideas. Twelve minds working together to get the job done. And when the task was too cumbersome for twelve, he pulled out a micro-team and headed for the mountaintop.

> After six days Jesus took with him Peter, James and John...and led them up a high mountain by themselves (Matthew 17:1).

Jesus asked for his team's input. He knew that giving it deepened their understanding. Seeking his disciples' feedback, Jesus asked:
"Have you understood all this?"
"What are others saying about me?"

"Who do you say that I am?"

"Are you able to drink the cup I am about to drink?"

Sometimes the team got the message; sometimes it didn't. On one occasion, the whole team quite literally missed the boat, causing Peter nearly to drown as he tried to walk on water. Of course, Jesus caught Peter and pulled him back in the boat. But as soon as the crisis had been averted, he stepped back and encouraged his team to rethink the situation. "Now, let's go over this again, guys…why did you doubt?"

Jesus was a master leader. As you prepare to lead your team, study Jesus' example. Then ask yourself the following questions:

• How can I follow Jesus' example as a servant leader?

• How will I verify that my instructions to team members have been heard and understood?

• How will I communicate to my team members that I value their ideas?

• How will I handle situations in which team members' ideas differ from my own?

• How will I nurture each team member's giftedness to strengthen the whole team?

Jesus and his disciples were a great team. Like all great teams, they frequently bounced their ideas off one another. Worship teams can do this too. As your team develops, you'll find yourself testing everyone's ideas in order to find out if they're worth keeping (the ideas—not the people). As Kenny Rogers sang in "The Gambler," "You got to know when to hold 'em, know when to fold 'em, know when to walk away and know when to run." Some ideas you'll hold tightly and "run with." Other ideas you'll drop immediately and run away from. And along the way somebody called the leader (that's you!) may have to decide which ideas are which. Remember that the buck stops with you, but only after you've consulted with your carefully recruited team.

PICKING THE PLAYERS

A great team requires great players. Each team member will come with unique strengths and weaknesses. However, our experience has shown that there are several traits that are "must-haves" for any worship design team member. Here are my "four F's" of great worship design team players:

Faith. No matter what the individual's role on the worship design team (videographer, drama writer, music director, or another position), his or her faith matters! The faith of great players must be active, vibrant, and passionate. These people must love Jesus! This kind of radical faith is described well in Michael Slaughter's book *Real Followers* (Nashville, TN: Abingdon Press, 1999).

Remember, this is the group who, along with the speaker, will help discern the best *word* from God for the weekend. It's impossible to squeeze blood out of a turnip, and it's equally impossible to squeeze faith-inspiring messages out of faith-challenged followers.

Flexibility. Let's face it, creative people are not necessarily known for their flexibility. Once we get these great ideas, we want to see them come to fruition! We love the thrill of knowing that a great worship experience developed out of *our* ideas. But when team players (or leaders, for that matter) "marry" their own ideas or ways of thinking, they may be hindered from finding the *best* idea. Great team players learn that while contributing an idea is good, seeing God work is *great*. And God works best when we collaborate on ideas. Teamwork, like family work, is a lot of give and take. It requires flexibility!

Future Picture. Unlike historians and art collectors whose job is to look back, worship design team players must always look forward. Great team players must always carry with them a picture of the next week's worship along with the motivation to find even better ways of connecting with participants. "Hey, why not?" must be their mantra. Often it will seem that change is the only constant in their lives. Therefore, team players must embrace and enjoy the next thing— the future picture.

Fit. I heard Barbara Walters describe the "team" on *The View* once. She noted that while they could interview and train many different types of women to sit on that couch, the key was *chemistry*. A great fit.

How do you find great fit? By examining how your team functions as a unit. Are your meeting times fixed or flexible? Are your existing team members on time or tardy? In meetings, do you update one another on personal or church news, or stick strictly to business? Do ideas flow freely, or do team members speak only when called upon? Each worship design team will have its own chemistry, or DNA. These are the characteristics that make your team unique and uniquely suited to minister within your particular church setting.

Our own team at Ginghamsburg is characterized by off-the-wall, ADD-ridden conversations. We have a common "sense of humor." We have fun together, but we also work hard. We have an almost uncanny ability to turn on a dime. When the need arises, we're able to pull together and fix our joint focus on the task at hand. Over time, we've established a comfortable intimacy level. While we lead very different lives, we all have strong egos that allow us to give and take compliments and criticism equally well.

At Ginghamsburg we use the Gallup StrengthsFinder tools, as found in the book *Now, Discover Your Strengths* (New York, NY: The Free Press of Simon & Schuster Inc., 2001), to help ensure that each team member is a good fit. This book includes an online survey that identifies an individual's top five strengths. The book also offers advice to enable individuals to use their strengths and to help team leaders manage them.

I highly recommend this resource to you and your team. It has enabled me to identify and understand my strengths as well as those of my entire team. I've discovered what sort of affirmation and helpful critique each team member needs. I'm learning what kind of communication speaks best and how each team member prefers to navigate change. Armed with this information, I can lead more effectively by interacting with each team member in more accommodating ways. My team members are learning to know and respect one another as well. This is the essence of a great team. We aren't necessarily best friends, but we truly enjoy working together and have learned to trust and respect one another's strengths.

To recap, great team players are
• faithfully following Jesus,
• flexibly offering creative ideas for consideration,
• fixing their focus on the future picture, and
• finding out where they fit in.

As team leader to these key players, your goal is to paint the biggest picture you can, then watch your team take it and run. When you give assignments to team players who meet these criteria, they'll often bring back more than you asked for. They'll consistently surprise you. They'll exceed the expectations. And you'll learn that you can trust them…with music selections, arrangements, video pieces, graphics, and countless other details.

Endnote

1. For more about Mike's "light-bulb moment," see Michael Slaughter, *Out on the Edge: A Wake-Up Call for Leaders on the Edge of the Media Reformation* (Nashville, TN: Abingdon Press, 1998).

CHAPTER 2

Finding Great Team Players

"Come, follow me,

and I will make you

fishers of men."

JESUS (MATTHEW 4:19)

Jesus called his team members out of unexpected vocations. Fishermen, tax collectors—not exactly the power team the religious leaders expected the Messiah to assemble. Perhaps some Pharisees grumbled at being excluded. But those unlikely disciples devoted themselves to Jesus and his mission, and together they got the job done.

In this chapter you'll learn where to look (think: unlikely places) and what to look for as you assemble your own worship design team. But before I suggest how to assemble a great team, I'll make a few suggestions about how *not* to go about it. I've learned these lessons the hard way!

LESSON 1: Do not invite staff persons simply because they wear a tie to work.

During my first day on this team, I was invited into a conference room full of pastoral staff. Most of them wore ties. One was desperately trying to learn media as a second career. The music director was present and pouting. I could have been intimidated and given up on the spot. But Mike Slaughter had a vision that I immediately connected with and embraced. While I had never received any formal training for what I envisioned could happen, it seemed that everything in my life up to that point had prepared me for this mission.

Initially, I joined the team as an occasional drama writer with a little experience as a musician and a visual designer. As our team dreams grew together, so did my passion for the cause. I worked without pay for a year and a half, then part-time for a very small salary. Eventually, I was hired full-time as team leader. The tie wearers eventually disinvited themselves to the meetings, and we began to acquire permission and direction to pursue new team players who shared the dream and demonstrated the passion and wiring to fully carry it out.

You may have "tie wearers" who want to have a say in your worship design. If so, gently encourage them to trust you to carry out your God-given dreams. Work hard; demonstrate your passion. If God has truly called you to this job, you'll eventually win them over.

LESSON 2: Do not assume all ordained clergy are passionate about the weekly worship experience.

Just because a clergy person has completed seminary does not mean that worship is his or her area of concentration or life passion. Your pastor may have focused his or her seminary training on discipleship, administration, counseling, or another aspect of church life. These other areas may be important to the life of your church, but they probably won't directly contribute to the well-being of your worship design team.

You can tell when a person has a different passion from worship design. He grows quiet and his eyes glaze over in a design team meeting. She asks to leave early because she needs to "work on a few other things." Do yourself and these folks a favor: Let them leave. Seek out like-minded people who are passionate about designing worship experiences.

LESSON 3: Do not invite people to join your team who simply agree with you and your ideas.

We all like to have our ideas affirmed. But remember, we're designing the most important hour in the week. Worship participants deserve the benefit of everyone's best thoughts. In order to achieve this, your team needs people who can think for themselves and speak those thoughts out loud. In our design team meetings here at Ginghamsburg, all contributions are highly esteemed. The more the better. Only after we've all thrown our thoughts out do we begin refining the focus.

From time to time we include interns in our worship design team meetings. Some interns just want to be in the room with us and do whatever we tell them to. This isn't nearly as helpful as the interns who speak up and say, "This is how I'm thinking about what you said," or "This is what God's showing me," or "Have you ever thought about doing thus and such?" That's an attitude I can work with, because it inspires all the members of the team to expand their thinking. Instead of making me feel better about myself, it makes everyone feel excited about the team.

LESSON 4: Do not assume that all great solo players are also star team players.

It's probably happened to you. You hear a great musician perform in a worship service and find yourself thinking, "Wouldn't it be great if we could get her on our worship team?" Maybe. It's possible that a great musician may be a wealth of inspiration to the music portion of your worship experience. But the same dose of self-confidence that enabled that performer to step out on stage may cause him or her to stubbornly hold on to ideas in team meetings.

Teamwork and solo work are different gifts. You may be lucky enough to find someone who can do both. If not, fill your team first with team players. You can invite soloists to fill meaningful parts in individual worship services. Worship design is a long-term, often behind-the-scenes commitment. Your team needs players who can shine whether or not they're in the limelight.

SO WHO DOES THAT LEAVE?

A great team comprises talented people who can spend a lot of time doing what they do best. When we've acquired new staff, paid or unpaid, we've learned to ask the "call" question. "What are you called to do? If money and time were not issues, what would you do with your life?" The people who serve on our team are absolutely passionate about worship. They are as dedicated to their area of service as they are to their day jobs (if they still have other day jobs).

By enlisting only team members who feel truly called to worship design, we've assembled a collection of mission-driven players whom we have to pressure to take vacations. "Sick time" can mean they make an extra trip to the bathroom during the workday. The only things sacred are family and personal re-creation time, for which most of us reserve Sunday noon through Tuesday mornings.

So who's on our team? At Ginghamsburg, our non-tie-wearing, passionate-about-worship, not-always-agreeable, put-the-team-first players include a music director, a videographer, a graphic designer, our weekend speaker (Mike, our

The difference between a team and a committee is that teams dream, develop, and deploy—*together.* Committees tell other people what to do but seldom hang around to see that the job gets done.

lead pastor, or someone else), and myself (as leader, writer, and often stage designer as well).

Our team is just that—a *team.* We're not a committee—and yes, there is a difference. The difference between a team and a committee is that teams dream, develop, and deploy—*together.* Committees tell other people what to do but seldom hang around to see that the job gets done. On our team, if you're in, you're in for the duration. Until the job gets done.

FISHING FOR TEAM MEMBERS

When Jesus called, his team members dropped everything and followed. For the rest of us, recruiting team members is a little more work. The task may seem daunting at first, but it's really not so scary if you know where to look.

When I've needed new team players, I've used what I call the "Stop, Look, and Listen" method of recruitment. For each team member you want to recruit, first *stop* and think. Think about how this person might look, think, and behave. Ask yourself, "In my wildest dreams, who is this person?"

Shortly after seeing Bobby McFerrin on a TV special, I found myself looking for a new band leader. Unrealistic as it was, Bobby McFerrin became my ideal as I stopped to consider the kind of person we needed to create a culturally diverse music ministry at Ginghamsburg. Did I really expect that we'd get Bobby McFerrin? Of course not. But in my wildest dreams we'd find a band leader with similar strengths.

Stop and dream a little about what kind of person you really want and need. Dreaming is a powerful way to move forward with our vision. Sometimes we're afraid to dream because we don't want to get excited and then have those dreams dashed when they don't come true. Quite the opposite is true, however. If we don't risk dreaming, we can never truly know and work toward a future picture. So have faith in your dreams. Dream big and write those dreams down. Entrust them to God and ask him to make them come true.

When you've dreamed all you can dream, it's time to *look*. Look in the places where you'd expect to find the kind of person you've been dreaming of. If you're looking for an eclectic musician (as I was), try looking in bands and clubs. Do a little research and find out where they're playing the kind of music you want to hear in your church. If you're looking for a videographer, check out local film schools and TV stations. Network with others in your church and community. Who knows? The team member you seek may be hidden right in your midst.

HELP WANTED

Funky, energetic, eclectic musician wanted for leadership position. Must love music more than life itself. Must love God more than music. Those experienced in church music need not apply.

When you think you may have found someone, then *listen*. Listen to what God is telling you to do, and obediently act on that direction. My best illustration of this comes out of a time when we were desperate for a strong female vocalist. I was pretty concerned about this and knew I had to *look* in every place I could. My husband Clark and I were at an outdoor street fair in the downtown of our little Tipp City. A band on the street was playing a rather eclectic mix of songs, and I heard the female vocalist say, "Turn that radio dial a little to the right, to the country station, and we'll do the next song."

It was evident that this singer had a diverse musical repertoire. At that moment, I felt my heart pounding and *listened* to God prod me to go speak to this woman about singing at Ginghamsburg Church. I only get that feeling every once in a while. When I do, I know I absolutely must scrape together the courage to act on the idea God has given me, or face the future left to my own pitiful devices.

Choosing the lesser of the two evils, I waited for the singer to take a break and then stepped out in obedience to what I believed was God's will. (Remember, I had no idea if this person had any faith background at all!) Heart pounding, I complimented her style and asked if she'd ever "thought about singing in a church." She smiled and replied that she'd love to sing in a church, but that it seldom paid the bills. Her smile spoke to me of her faith potential. I responded, "If I promise to pay your bills, will you come sing with us at Ginghamsburg Church sometime soon?" She said that she would. I followed up with a phone call, and she sang with us a few weeks later.

I remember that weekend, planning the music with the bandleader and the team. I told the team about a new singer I'd met and scheduled. I didn't talk it up much, just trusted and asked that her first song be "Worship You." That Saturday night, this vocalist walked out onto center stage at the beginning of our worship celebration and delivered that song, a cappella at first, and then really wailing it with all the stops pulled out, accompanied by the band.

Needless to say, that Saturday evening our congregation had a huge God experience, and Cheryl Wyatt joined our band. I was excited that God had given us a much-needed servant. Cheryl's faith and passion for Jesus are gifts that have truly blessed our church over and over again.

A few months later, we found ourselves in need of a full-time bandleader and discovered that Cheryl's husband, Francis, was a professional musician as well. We promptly invited Fran to join us and now refer to him fondly as "the human percussionist." Fran's uniquely diverse music and his personal mission of people restoration have become powerful threads in the fabric of Ginghamsburg. Fran's faith reaches many people in ministry each weekend through his music and passion. I shiver to think what would have happened if I had not *listened* and acted on God's voice that evening in downtown Tipp City.

Finding a worship leader at a street fair? (Finding disciples in a fishing boat…) Who would have thought it could happen? To inspire your search, here are a few other unlikely places where we've found team members.

Interning at Area Television Stations

Todd Carter, our chief videographer, was a student at Cedarville University when he met his future wife, Kari, who attended Ginghamsburg. Todd was a natural-born media lover (he remembers watching cartoons from his crib) and had studied and interned at area television stations. When an associate media director position was posted in our church bulletin, Todd applied. Todd's solid integrity and ability to ensure the God focus in every story makes him an extremely valuable team player.

Studying at Local Colleges

Worship and Web graphic artist Brent Thurston has had an amazing life journey of experiences as a missionary's kid in Hong Kong, Christian high school back in the States, and then Cincinnati Bible College. While in college, Brent picked up on his dorm mate's interest in computer art and transferred to Dayton's Sinclair Community College to study graphic arts. One of our staff discovered Brent at his graduate art show while "sniffing around" for a potential team player…a match made in heaven.

PLAYING WITH OTHER MUSICIANS

Fran met Tom Lipps, our resident keyboardist, when they were called to play the same jazz gig in downtown Dayton. While Tom is a devoted Catholic, his true desire is to use his life and his music to build a bridge between faith communities. Now a huge asset to our band, Tom is another match made in heaven. Outside gigging can create powerful networks and relationships for growing a band, and Tom is proof of the value of that kind of connection.

It's essential to expand our thinking about where to find great team players. Concerts, schools, art shows, other churches and denominations, and the basic networking of existing team members are all possible sources for the people you need. Cast your net far and wide—you'll be surprised at the team members you might pull in.

Stop, look, and *listen* to find your best team players. Be bold in your dreams! Step out and explore!

ASSIMILATING YOUR CATCH

You've dreamed your dreams, cast your net (over and over, it seems), and you think you have the makings of a great team. Now what? Once you've found your team players, you'll want to solidify their roles on the team. You may have used a written job description as a guide while you were recruiting your team members. Now that everyone is on board, it's time to do a reality check. People seldom come to us in the exact packages we prescribe. With your job description in one hand, and a team member's résumé (formal or informal) in the other, ask yourself: How can I maximize this person's gifts? What skills is he or she missing? Are those skills somewhere else on the team? If so, where? If not, how can I help this person acquire them?

Written job descriptions can be found on the following pages for each of the Ginghamsburg team players described in this chapter. Use them as they are, adapt them to your setting, or reflect on them as inspiration to create your own unique documents as you assemble your team.

POSITION: Creative Director

ACCOUNTABLE TO: Director of Ministries or Lead Pastor

Position Requirements
- Serve as participating player on the Senior Management Team in order to connect the church's mission and DNA into the worship experience
- Serve as leader of the Worship Design Team
- Demonstrated ability to motivate, coordinate, and lead creative worship development, resulting in powerful worship experiences
- Demonstrated ability to plan and execute large events and conferences

Spiritual Qualifications
- Professes Jesus Christ as Lord and Savior
- Committed to personal spiritual growth and healthy lifestyle
- Considers this position primary ministry and occupation
- Models standards and expectations of leaders within the church, including
  - participation in a cell group
  - living a lifestyle of tithing and generosity
  - serving faithfully out of call and giftedness

Education/Experience
- Proven competence, insight, and creative grasp of multiple communication forms, including spoken word, written word, music, media, and drama
- Degree in an area such as communications, theater, English, journalism, or marketing, or equivalent life experience
- Experience in theater, music, speech, and writing helpful

Skills
- Ability to "dream ahead" and oversee events, environment, and worship gatherings within church ministry setting
- Ability to translate overall church DNA into various ministry environments throughout church facilities, much as an interior designer would do for a home
- Ability to team with strategic partners to ensure maximum quality for all products, communications, and events

Position: **Music Director**

Accountable to: Creative Director (may be accountable to pastor or associate pastor in smaller churches)

Position Requirements
- Oversee music churchwide
- Recruit, train, and mentor leaders for adult bands as well as student and children's ministry areas as needed
- Serve as an active player on the Worship Design Team
- Lead and connect effectively with congregation based on pastor/leader's vision in overall weekly worship experience

Spiritual Qualifications
- Professes Jesus Christ as Lord and Savior
- Committed to personal spiritual growth and healthy lifestyle
- Considers this position primary ministry
- Models standards and expectations of leaders within the church, including
  - participating in a cell group
  - living a lifestyle of tithing and generosity
  - serving faithfully out of call and giftedness

Education/Experience
- Formal training or college degree in instrumental or vocal music, or equivalent life experience
- Experience in broad variety of settings with a wide scope of musical styles

Skills
- Musically talented and magnetic stage personality
- Ability to arrange music and use related software effectively
- Organized work habits (or ability to partner with strategic assistant)
- Effective relationship skills

POSITION: **Videographer**

ACCOUNTABLE TO: Creative Director or Operations Manager

Position Requirements
- Cast vision and ensure churchwide media quality based on leader's vision
- Ability to attract, motivate, and train teams of unpaid servants to deploy media ministry churchwide
- Serve as an active player on the Worship Design Team
- Demonstrate ability to dream, develop, and deploy all media-related pieces for worship, conferencing, and discipleship ministry as needed
- Assess, purchase, and care for all media equipment churchwide

Spiritual Qualifications
- Professes Jesus Christ as Lord and Savior
- Committed to personal spiritual growth and healthy lifestyle
- Considers this position primary ministry and occupation
- Models standards and expectations of leaders within the church, including
  - participating in a cell group
  - living a lifestyle of tithing and generosity
  - serving faithfully out of call and giftedness

Education/Experience
- Degree in communications, media, broadcast, or related field, or equivalent life experience
- Proficiency in all forms of media
- Proven ability to translate the gospel through media usage

Skills
- Effective team leader
- Effective team player
- Passion to grow and incorporate new methods and media forms

POSITION: **Graphic Arts Specialist**

ACCOUNTABLE TO: Creative Director, Media Director, or Operations Manager

Position Requirements
- Work closely with key staff communicators in order to understand and translate concepts, information, and inspiration into visually effective images
- Serve as an active player on the Worship Design Team
- Serve as participating player on other teams (discipleship, Web, print communications, etc.) as needed

Spiritual Qualifications
- Professes Jesus Christ as Lord and Savior
- Committed to personal spiritual growth and healthy lifestyle
- Considers this position primary ministry and occupation
- Models standards and expectations of leaders within the church, including
  - participating in a cell group
  - living a lifestyle of tithing and generosity
  - serving faithfully out of call and giftedness

Education/Experience
- Bachelor's or associate's degree from graphic arts or tech school, or equivalent life experience
- Proficiency in graphic arts, print, and screen
- Working knowledge of wide variety of related software (Adobe Photoshop, Microsoft Photo Editor, and others)
- Proven ability to translate spiritual concepts into visual images

Skills
- Effective team player
- Strategic use of time and resources
- Passion to grow and learn new methods, styles, and software
- Proven artistic talent for translating DNA of organization

CHAPTER 3

The Vital Role of the Pastor-Speaker

"It was he who gave some to be apostles, some to be prophets, some to be evangelists, and some to be pastors and teachers."

PAUL (EPHESIANS 4:11)

C reativity is a wonderful thing. Week after week, the creative juices flow as our worship design team endeavors to craft the weekend worship celebrations. Remarkably, we are continually blessed with new ideas to help worship participants experience God in fresh ways. If our worship celebrations were exactly the same week after week, I'd worry that we'd all died and gone to hell. (Fortunately, since they don't hold worship celebrations in hell, this is not likely to actually happen.) Without creativity, all of the life would go out of our worship.

But worship experiences don't come to life out of human creativity alone. As a worship designer, I like to define creativity this way:

> Creativity is the empowered ability to carry out any endeavor using all the rich resources that God has made available.

In order for our creativity to be effective, it must point to the Creator. Our creative efforts must be a visible indication of the invisible God. A worship design team's creative work must point to a source much greater than the team members themselves, and someone has to introduce that source. Someone has to bring the word of God into each worship celebration's message, and that "someone" is usually the pastor or speaker.

> The Word became flesh and made his
> dwelling among us (John 1:14).

THE WORD AMONG US

Each week, as we design powerful worship experiences, I'm convinced that we are truly making space for the Word to come and dwell among us. At Ginghamsburg that means one person must put that Word into words for the team. The team can suggest points, titles, additional scriptures, stories, songs, dramas, and metaphors, but the "Word" must be central for transformation to occur in the lives of participants.

Mike Slaughter is our primary teacher at Ginghamsburg. Mike's not known for being particularly easy to work with, overly friendly, or adaptable. He's more prophet than organizational genius and can occasionally infuriate his teammates. (Prophets often forget to check the popularity polls!) But Mike is a passionate team player. And at 9:15 Wednesday morning we can count on him to show up in room 202 with his Bible and yellow pad, ready to share the word from God with the worship design team. Every Wednesday, without fail.

The word Mike brings us isn't just a little piece of Scripture or a few ideas for points. This "word" is a life-changing, huge, hairy, audacious premise based in Scripture, that when drawn out to its full extent will transform its hearers. Participants who experience this word will commit to being passionate Jesus-followers or be exposed as religious pretenders. As we "chew on" this word together as a team, the word must hook us, intrigue us, provoke us, and motivate us. If there is no tension with the message, the team doesn't feel it's worship-worthy.

In 2 Timothy 4:2, Paul charges Timothy, "Preach the Word; be prepared in season and out of season; correct, rebuke and encourage—with great patience and careful instruction." As our lead teacher, Mike takes this exhortation very seriously, and so does the rest of our team. Ephesians 6:17 refers to God's word as "the sword of the Spirit." At Ginghamsburg, we are fully aware that God's word, spoken through Mike, will pierce the hearts and souls of worship participants. It will convict them and spur them on to follow Jesus in exciting and powerful ways. Even in a multisensory worship service such as ours, the Word needs to drive the worship. Everything else we do must support and enhance it.

Debbie Kasper, a Lutheran clergyperson and fellow worship designer, visited

Ginghamsburg recently to observe our worship design team. I asked Debbie to share her feedback with me after she returned home. I was interested in what her "fresh eyes" might observe about our worship environment and overall design process. I'll share more of her comments in Chapter 10, but here's what she had to say about Mike's teaching.

> *I was taken with the preparedness of the sermon by Friday. So many pastors are still writing on Friday. I was impressed with the level of detail Mike had by then. I also felt the sermon walk-through on Saturday was critical considering the amount of detailing you do for the stories.*
>
> *Mike is a very inspirational preacher. He's interesting in that he is a cross between boomer and postmodern in his preaching style. Boomer in two ways: the three-point sermon and the speaker as leader in providing answers to life's problems. (For most postmoderns, the speaker is a fellow journeyer, asking questions more than giving answers, offering options. Neither is better than the other, just different styles.) He is postmodern in his storytelling capabilities and his relational presence on stage. He is extremely likeable, friendly, and real on stage.*

Churches will take on the passion, DNA, and initiatives of their leaders. Ginghamsburg is a church targeted toward twenty-five- to forty-five-year-olds who have children in the home and who have been turned off or out by traditional churches. We seek to be an authentic, culturally diverse community producing radical followers of Jesus Christ. This is our call from God as identified through Mike as our lead pastor. The weekend messages are simply the most effective way to present the vision and give clarity to the mission. That is why the role of the pastor is vital to the design process. We *become* these messages.

MESSAGES WITHOUT A MESSENGER?

We always have a number of weekends a year that Mike is not involved in worship as the speaker. On these weekends, we must find the messenger so the message can find us! To fill in the gaps, I schedule a variety of speakers, some from within Ginghamsburg (even from our team) and others from the larger faith community. The key is that we never ask someone whom we doubt will bring a powerful word from God to us.

Each "speaker" must share his or her word Wednesday morning, whether by phone, fax, e-mail attachment, or in person. We "push" the word as a team, even in the speaker's absence if need be, until the word seems powerful to us. Having a change of speakers allows for greater diversity and creative opportunities, which serves our mission well. We love the guest speakers and the fresh word they bring. But no one knows the hearts of our people like Mike, and we always appreciate him even more when he returns.

We are so fortunate to have Mike's intimate involvement with our team. My heart goes out to those worship teams who must soldier on without this strong level of support, for deep down I know that God works best through committed leadership. Yet every time I present at a worship conference, it seems that at least one person will privately share his or her discouragement over the pastor's lack of involvement. They are passionate about worship, they tell me, and deeply desire that God would move in their church community. But their pastor will not meet with their team or comes to worship team meetings unprepared. What to do?

I tell these folks to talk to their pastors and assure them that they aren't trying to take over the worship experience. I encourage them to affirm the ultimate importance of the pastor's spoken word. I suggest that they share their vision for worship, where the Word guides the pastor and worship team to work together to create God experiences that engage participants with all their senses. When approached with humility and grace, many pastors will catch the vision and come around.

However, it's possible that the pastor will refuse. If I found myself in that situation, I would pray hard and seek God's direction, but not give up my God-given worship dreams. I know deep down that I've been wired to serve where my passions and abilities are embraced, and I would continue to pray and move toward that end—even if it meant finding another church. Life is too short to spend our best days "wrestling against flesh and blood" (Ephesians 6:12, New King James Version).

The teaching and speaking aspect of the pastor's role is extremely vital. Small word—small worship. Big word—big, huge, incredible worship! In order for this kind of synergy to take place, the pastor must stay ahead of his or her people in spirit and in truth. Mike rises at 5:30 each morning to be with God, pray, and study related Scriptures and writings in order to fulfill this call. Several months after I first began serving on the design team, I boldly stated that I would stay with this mission as long as Mike stayed ahead of me. While we all bring diverse strengths to the table, Mike has demonstrated consistent spiritual strength…and I am still here.

Happy are the people whose God is the Lord and who have assurance that the *Word* will be incarnated uniquely each week in worship.

CHAPTER 4

Small Churches Empowering Teams That Soar

"Without faith it is impossible to please God."

(HEBREWS 11:6)

When I speak at conferences about multisensory worship, at least one pastor or worship leader will usually raise a hand and ask, "If you were just starting out designing worship [whether it's because the church is small, young, or just received a wake-up call], how would you do it?" Because the multisensory worship at Ginghamsburg is now well-established, listeners just assume that it's always been that way. But we had to start somewhere. At one time, we were where they are, and we continue to refine the model. In fact, for the last eight years, our worship center has been a research and development laboratory where we've tried at least one new thing almost every single weekend.

When I first began working on the worship design team at Ginghamsburg, the stage was large, but the worship celebration was fairly predictable. A randomly selected staff person offered a welcome, prayer, Scripture, and announcements; a choir sang enthusiastically to CD track accompaniments; a couple of music lovers led a few worship songs; and Mike always delivered a great message. Despite media capability, the screen was blank the majority of the time. (My two pet peeves: blank screens and unlit candles. Both say, "The door is open, but nobody's home!")

To make things worse, the congregation, like their Israelite ancestors in faith, wanted to go back to Egypt. "Egypt" for us was our old, cramped church building where seats, parking spots, and bathroom privileges were always in short supply. Nothing felt polished, and no one felt compelled to look or sound "professional." Back in Egypt, everyone could feel God's presence, because we were so crowded we had to *feel* something!

But a new day was dawning at Ginghamsburg. We had reached the Promised Land, and a new, much larger building was ours to fill. But finding the best ways to use the new facility was a challenge—in the beginning. As Jesus noted early in his ministry, you can't put new wine into old wineskins. We still wanted to enjoy the richness of worship celebrations we'd experienced before, but we needed new wineskins to enjoy them in.

Slowly but surely, we began to think in new ways. First order of business: Use the screen as a modern-day stained-glass window. We needed to get *something* inspirational up on that screen. We continued to dream of ways we could fill up the stage, warm up the room, and enhance the space with music that inspired. What we needed was multisensory worship—multimedia that helped tell the stories and music that reflected the growing multicultural passion in our hearts. But where would we start? This is the challenge of many churches desiring to step out and start growing, and it was our challenge as well.

> As Jesus noted early in his ministry, you can't put new wine into old wineskins. We still wanted to enjoy the richness of worship celebrations we'd experienced before, but we needed new wineskins to enjoy them in.

BEGINNING...

Our dramas began with yours truly doing monologues, then asking others to join me—one talented person at a time. Our band began with a single keyboard player and gradually added drums, guitar, bass, percussion, and sometimes extra instruments. We created our first screen graphics by simply scanning freehand sketches or copyright-free illustrations. When we wanted to add media, we purchased a CVLI (Christian Video Licensing International) license for a modest annual fee. The CVLI license allows us to show video clips from movies. This has become an effective part of our multisensory worship. (For more information about the CVLI license, or to obtain one for your church, see http://www.mplc.com/index2.htm.)

How do you get started? The answer for any new worship endeavor is not to scale down your dreams, but rather to simplify your strategy and build those dreams while you...

Take One Small Step at a Time

> Then Peter got down out of the boat,
> walked on the water and came toward
> Jesus. But when he saw the wind, he
> was afraid and, beginning to sink,
> cried out, "Lord, save me!"
> (Matthew 14:29-30).

No one knew small steps better than Peter. Peter was a fragile human being with a bit of a crazy streak, but he knew enough to realize that faith can't grow in the context of comfort. As Peter and the disciples saw the ghostlike figure approaching on the water, they panicked. Was it Jesus? Or was it really a ghost?

There were only two possible outcomes to that scenario. Either it really *was* Jesus walking toward their boat, and he would eventually make it to them safe and sound; or it was a ghost, and that ghost would eventually come close enough to scare the bejeebers out of them. Either way, Peter's stepping out of the boat was not going to help! There was no good reason for him to step out of the boat that stormy night. He was safe with his buddies in the boat, and Jesus was already walking toward them. Why get out?

I think it was the child in Peter that wanted to get his own piece of the action. Perhaps Peter was a kinesthetic learner. Maybe he knew that if he could feel the power of the wind around him and the roll of the waves beneath him, he'd be onto something bigger than life. He'd experience God firsthand; he'd get a piece of the God action. The very thought of it invigorated him. He couldn't just sit in the boat pondering what would happen—he had to get out and try it! So Peter stood up and called out to the figure in the distance, "Lord, if it's you, tell *me* to come to *you* on the water" (Matthew 14:28).

Designing powerful worship experiences in a smaller church will definitely take everyone involved out of their comfortable, dry boat and into the storm. You'll feel the wind around you and the rolling waves under you, but one day you'll be the last to leave that little church building after a powerful God experience...and you'll be sure you're walking on water.

As you step out in obedience to fulfill your God-given worship dreams, your faith will grow, and the faith (and possibly the size!) of your congregation will too. Remember that without faith, it's impossible to please God. We all need to be taking on projects and ministry endeavors that can succeed only with the help of God, with the exercise of faith.

You can begin by asking yourself what one small step you'll take. You know you'll have to get out of the boat, but what will be your first step onto the water? Will you recruit one musician to develop a band? Will you ask one person to write or perform a drama? Will you take ten minutes today to assess your technology needs as they relate to worship? Do it now and you'll be on your way.

> We all need to be taking on projects and ministry endeavors that can succeed only with the help of God, with the exercise of faith.

Keep It Simple

Small churches *can* empower teams that soar. Working simple allows for more ministry impact using fewer people. You don't have to have a huge team of paid staff. You just have to cover all your bases. Start simply with a small team of three or four people who can cover the following key worship design team positions.

heart | soul | mind | strength

Musician—Look for a key musician who can envision, arrange, and perform the style(s) of music that would best enhance your church's vision and attract its target audience. (If you haven't defined a target audience, now's the time to ask yourself, "What kinds of people attend our church?") Music is a key component in worship design. So as you begin, it's critical to match your music style(s) to the musical tastes of those most likely to be attracted to the church and its preaching style.

As you search for musicians, remember: It's easier to disciple a great musician who has named Jesus as Lord than to teach an adult disciple to make great music. The key musician on a worship team must have proven musical talent. Ideally, he or she should practice and play music regularly. Regular playing produces quality music, and it also attracts quality musicians. Musicians who play regularly know other musicians—possibly even right in your church.

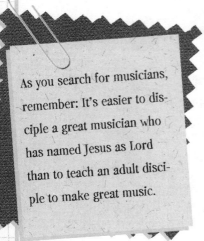

Share your worship dreams with your key musician. Work together to define a musical style that will fit your church. Then charge your key musician with the mission of building a band or music ministry out of his or her own network and the church family. Encourage him or her to *start simple*, but with *high quality*. Think: If we build it (beautifully), they will come. People are attracted to that which inspires.

Technician—To succeed in multisensory worship, you'll need a technical guru who can run a projector and a sound system. "Anything is possible with duct tape," this person will affirm. The technician is a support personality who feels passionately that "if we speak with the tongues of men and angels, but have not the right equalization on the vocal mics, or the screen is dark, we are *nothing*."

By all means, share your vision with your technician. While a technician on the worship design team may not be required to articulate your mission, he or she should definitely understand and support it. After all, his or her skills will be critical in helping you realize it.

Word Weaver—The word weaver is someone who can grasp the message and translate it, drawing people into the experience in a variety of ways. Dramatic pieces, prayers, calls to worship, and even announcements must all support the weekly word. Initially your pastor may fill this role, but it will eventually be helpful to identify someone else who can take that load off the primary speaker and consider this a ministry in its own right.

Stage Designer—The stage designer sets both the physical stage and, perhaps more importantly, the "spiritual stage." The physical stage includes any props, visuals, or set pieces you'll be using (for more about setting the physical stage, see Chapter 10). The spiritual stage is the tone or atmosphere you're seeking to create with each unique worship celebration. The stage designer is a visual thinker who understands what it means to provide an ambience that whispers, "I have prepared a place for you...you are welcome here...the Spirit is alive and present...relax and be in the moment with God."

As with the preceding players I've described, the stage designer doesn't have to be a paid staff person, and elaborate stage design is not often needed. But having the right person in this position can make all the difference. Carefully placed candles, thoughtfully selected background images, and mood-setting choices of color and texture all come together to draw worshippers in. The stage designer's own home ambience is usually confirmation of his or her passion to create spiritual spaces and an environment of expectation. It's a true God moment when a potential stage designer comes to realize that his or her gift for ambience setting can be used to advance God's kingdom.

> The stage designer is a visual thinker who understands what it means to provide an ambience that whispers, "I have prepared a place for you...you are welcome here...the Spirit is alive and present...relax and be in the moment with God."

To form a simple, small team, all you need are these four positions: musician, technician, word weaver, and stage designer. If you're lucky, you may find someone in your midst who's wired to fulfill more than one role. Or you may get "two for the price of one" and find a couple or group who'd like to share responsibility for a position. Each church setting will offer its own unique variety of personalities, and it's exciting to see how different churches have configured their teams. Perhaps no other church will do it quite the way you do!

Seek Only Mission-Driven People

As you begin to assemble your team, resolve now to seek only mission-driven people. Worship design is not a job for those seeking prestige or comfort. These positions are for people who show up to serve because they love doing their piece. You think about paying them only when you can no longer afford for them to keep their day jobs and the church's growth is such that they've generated their own salaries.

During my first year on the team, I was told that this would *never* be a paying job. That did not seriously deter me, however. I loved doing what I'd

been created to do, and eventually the mission required my presence more often than my day job would allow. As I devoted more and more time to worship design, the worship celebrations continued to grow in attendance and effectiveness.

Simply put, mission-driven people faithfully and passionately fulfill their given roles not for money, prestige, or out of a sense of duty, but for the love of what they do. The ultimate desire of a mission-driven person is to see the project come to magnificent fruition—to witness changed lives and to say, "I had a part in that." Mission-driven people are real followers of Jesus, serving to make an eternal difference in their own lives and the lives of those around them. You need these people on your team.

EMPOWERING...

It is the task of any paid staff to support and ensure the success of the unpaid team players. These critical, unpaid players must receive first-hand information on the message they are to enhance. They must work with reliable, focused staffers who will carry out any strategic functions that, for whatever reason, only paid persons can do.

Part of ensuring the success of any team players, whether paid or unpaid, is to be a leader in three important ways: Stay in touch, communicate the vision, and connect the team members.

Stay in Touch Regularly

Schedule team meetings regularly at a mutually agreed-upon time. Most teams will meet at least weekly, but your meeting schedule should match the organizational style of your team. Whatever schedule you choose, remember that meeting times must be at the convenience of the unpaid servants, and the importance of those meetings cannot be overestimated. In addition to meetings, you may need to follow up with various team members via phone or e-mail.

Communicate the Vision Continually

Take the opportunity to paint the bigger picture as the team deals with decisions, challenges, and questions. Check in with individual team members regularly to ensure that each player understands the vision and his or her part in carrying it out. Provide opportunities for team members to do what they love to do in the context of worship development. Point the way to any additional ministry opportunities in your church or community that might help team members to hone and sharpen their gifts.

Connect Team Members Creatively

No team member (including you, the leader) can do everything perfectly. We all need strategic partnerships to support us in our weaker areas. I tend to be a big-picture person. I need others around me who can provide dedicated attention to the details of a specific project. When I'm asked to design a new meeting room environment at Ginghamsburg, I always seek the help of a project manager and a second creative design partner. Encourage your team members to look first to one another, then to the larger church community, to find the help they need to get the job done.

> Two are better than one, because they have a good return for their work (Ecclesiastes 4:9).

SOARING!

Once you've gathered your key players and organized them into a functioning team, you're ready to soar. To inspire you, here is a letter I received a year ago from a kindred spirit, a fellow worship designer working with a new worship service in an older, established church. I asked how they were doing, and this was her response:

Kim,

We are doing really well, but the team is exhausted. No one warned us (or we didn't listen) about the volume of work that was involved, and we're all volunteers at this point. The service is growing at a steady pace (five to ten new people a week), and those that come really seem to be moved by what we are doing.

As for the multisensory part, we move the service within the building. We are fortunate to have both an adaptable sanctuary as well as a multi-use fellowship hall. People have to come to the church on Sunday nights to find out where the service will be held that week. We pick the space as a team, based on the configuration of the service (what components we are including that week), how large the band is for the night, and other activities within the church. One week we even moved within the building during the service. It was about the Garden and submitting to God, so we actually walked through our Meditation Garden as part of the service, then ended the walk in front of an oversized wooden cross. It was really very moving, not just in the literal sense.

We have a band that moves from rock to jazz, from folk to pop to gospel, and they adapt the music to the needs of the service. We use movie clips to teach about discipleship. We have a team that dances about once every eight weeks. We pick our themes a little farther in advance than you do, so we can find a song that works well with our theme. Then we give them to our artist in residence and she choreographs a number. We also use a great deal of drama, almost on a weekly basis.

The space that we worship in changes each week too. For a communion service entitled "Gather at the Table," we actually set up tables in the worship space and had people gather and worship around them. Then we served communion to each other at the table. We've strung lights from the ceiling, draped material over all of the chairs to simulate water, and often give people a gift when they leave. The week we did "Hope," we gave out [flower] bulbs. The week we talked about being where God needs you, we gave out puzzle pieces. When we spoke on money, we gave everyone a penny.

I hope this gives you an idea of what we're doing.

May God pour His richest blessings upon you and all that you work with.

Shalom,
Amy

Amy's team was just starting out, all unpaid. But she moved forward with her vision, and as a result, worship participants were moved toward God. Can you sense the excitement in store for you as your worship design team takes flight?

I checked in with Amy again a year later to find out what this weekly process of creating multisensory worship has taught her and her team. This is what Amy had to say:

Kim,

Thank you so much for asking about our progress; it has been quite a year. Here are the most important lessons that we have learned over the last year of doing this weekly service:

• It is going to take a lot more time and energy than you plan on it taking! In the beginning, we struggled to do just about everything. As we became more comfortable and gained some experience, we were able to do things better, but a big service like Christmas Eve will still take weeks to get ready. The whole team will put in a great deal of work.

• It is going to cost more money than you planned on. We've been struggling with money from the beginning and will most likely continue to in the future because we have really big dreams…and they cost money.

• An organizational plan is everything. Because of my background (a bachelor's degree in religion with minors in music and drama, and a master's in social administration), I knew that process was the most vital piece of making this service go. We developed a time line and an implementation process that we've tweaked in the last year, but for the most part it is the same. Each service is planned over a four-week period; at any given time, the team should know where the service is within the planning phase.

• You have to be flexible! Twice in the last year we've decided a few days before the service that we needed to comment on something that was happening (in the culture) right then. We needed to write a service in a few days, which was more difficult, but we produced some of our best services because of it.

• Thank people for their time and effort. Since everyone is a volunteer, it is really important to thank people for the time they've put in. Whether it is a lay preacher that we have for one week, the service host, or one of the technicians who serve once a month, everyone is thanked for their time and effort with (at least) a hand-written note and sometimes a small gift.

• If you are going to go out there with your worship, you have to be prepared to fail. We've been highly experimental with our worship, and sometimes it's been really wonderful. There was a time when the whole congregation gathered around the children that were being baptized and sang "Jesus Loves Me." The family joined as a whole to show that we all share in the responsibility of raising the children. But it can also be really bad—like when we were trying to have people light candles before communion. They just did not know where to go, and we ended up with a big pile of people.

• God brought us all together in this time and in this place. And for that (no matter how difficult or frustrating) we should be thankful and full of praise. This is a gift and a blessing for us all.

We have learned so much in the last year. As we move into our second full year, we have a great deal more confidence and composure than we had at the same point last year. There is a great deal of excitement, and after the summer off, we are ready to get back to work. We've made a concerted effort to do more publicity this year; advertising is important, and we are addressing the need to understand that our congregation is going to come from people who are not currently being served and from those who are outside of the current church structure.

May God bless you and keep you and your team joyful.

Shalom,

Amy

Small churches and new, fledgling starts *can* empower teams that soar. There's just something crazily exciting the first time you realize that you've created something powerful together. Take one step at a time, keep it simple, seek only mission-driven people, and be or find a leader who will support and work to ensure the success of unpaid staff. You just may find yourself walking on water!

PART TWO:
At Home With the Ginghamsburg Team

When I was young, I loved going over to my friends' homes and just hanging out. No matter what we did, the best part for me was getting a look inside that family...seeing how they interacted...experiencing the space they called "home." I was always curious about the "inside story" of everyday human beings.

In much the same way, many people have expressed curiosity about the "inside story" of the Ginghamsburg worship team. Some have heard me speak at worship conferences; others have attended worship celebrations at Ginghamsburg. These inquiring minds want to see behind the scenes of our worship experience. What do our design meetings look like? How do we dream as a team?

In the next three chapters, I'll take you through a typical (if there is such a thing) week in the life of our team. You'll get a feel for the way we work as a team, and the way our team works within our church. We hope the following chapters and the behind-the-scenes video on the enclosed DVD will make you feel welcome in our "home." Think of it as a home show: Come on in, look around, and take away lots of dreams for your home worship team.

CHAPTER 5

Anatomy of a Design Team Meeting

"Nothing happens

unless first a dream."

CARL SANDBURG

It's 9:15 Wednesday morning. Design team players are beginning to gather in room 202 upstairs at Ginghamsburg. The room is about 15x15, and four standard, rectangular folding tables have been set up to create a large square table for this assembly. The chairs are comfortable, but not cozy. As a team, we've somewhat reluctantly settled on a room that lacks ambience. However, the lack of atmosphere is balanced by the room's capability to "log on" with multiple laptops. We're wired and ready to get down to business!

> Doctor appointments must be scheduled for other days. Time off or other ministry meetings must be at other times. To be on this team means to be at this meeting.

Looking around the room, you'll see a large whiteboard on the wall. Listening, you'll hear the sounds of preschool children's play floating up from the worship area "playground" below. Fresh, hot coffee and water await our consumption. Regular team players, subs, and interns have come together to do what we've sought to do every week for eight years—design an unforgettable, powerful weekend worship experience.

Designing worship that will bring the Word to our congregation is our mission, and this is where it all begins. This means that the weekly design team meeting is of the highest priority. The team leader, pastor, musician(s), technician(s), word weaver(s), and stage designer(s) for the upcoming worship celebration must all be present to design as a team. Doctor appointments must be scheduled for other days. Time off or other ministry meetings must be at other times. To be on this team means to be at this meeting. On vacation? You can send in your replacement, who has been trained to be "you" all week long. Nothing else should be planned until at least three o'clock in the afternoon. This meeting time is so important that we don't even break for lunch. We've asked an administrative support person to come in, take our lunch orders and money (we all have to agree on a restaurant), and go fetch lunch (or call for delivery) for us to eat in room 202. If we took a break, we'd lose our train of thought and our momentum. (Remember our ADD component.)

Designing worship is the best and worst part of the week. My prayers to God on Wednesday morning are a mixture of anxiety and expectancy as I prepare for what lies ahead. It's great fun to create such an event together, yet it's very hard work to design an awesome God experience every seven days, fifty-two times a year. As draining as they are, I'm grateful for our weekly marathon meetings. Teams working with all unpaid servants have to be even *more* strategic, perhaps planning on a weekday evening and possibly *not* every week. A lot of teams have to plan a month at a time or a series at a time and simply convene weekly to solidify the upcoming weekend celebration. For us, we meet every Wednesday, all day long, to dream.

WARM-UP

Back to room 202: We are comfortably settling in. As you see in the behind-the-scenes DVD segment, the guys are all working on their laptops. We are now ready to debrief the previous weekend's celebrations. But alas, we have already gotten off to a tangential start, discussing who saw what movie, why it was really, really bad (or really, really good), whose software needs to be updated, whose recent vacation was boring or cool, how the kids are, how the parents are, and so on. Lots of teasing and "team" jokes go on here. Perhaps this is the kind of lighthearted, relaxing atmosphere humans need when faced with daunting tasks. If our meetings were all business, we'd eventually burn out.

DEBRIEF

After the warm-up, we debrief. I remind the team of the worship elements from the previous weekend (the three days that have passed since Sunday offer plenty of forgetting time!). We ask ourselves what we felt worked, how the congregation connected, and whether anyone has heard reports about the experience from outside the team circle. We always try to identify elements with which people connected and times they may have been disconnected or distracted. Our debriefing includes everything from message delivery to technical details. Listen in:

> "I liked the 'reader's theater' in the middle of the opening song."
>
> "I did, too, but we shouldn't do it again for a while. We've done that twice in a month's time."
>
> "Yeah, I know. It just seemed to fit so well."
>
> "Wonder why we go in streaks like that?"
>
> "Speaking of streaks, all the music last weekend had a very 'white' vibe. Did you notice that?"
>
> "No, the offering song had a Latin feel."
>
> "True, but the worship music was way vanilla."
>
> "Good point. Let's be sure to work up some gospel or R & B this week. We've got a large vocal ensemble scheduled."
>
> "Mike's message hit home for some people. I think others might have needed more definite action steps. Not everyone thinks in concepts, you know."
>
> "Let's keep pushing the action steps part of the message then. You're right. A lot of people really want bottom line."
>
> "I heard action steps!"
>
> "Well, we can keep pushing it anyway. How was the music mix in the house?"
>
> "Good on the floor but a little weak in the balcony. Sure wish we could afford some extra horns."
>
> "Not a good time right now. Let's put it on the wish list."

Remember the Gallup StrengthsFinder tools I described in Chapter 1? Well, one of my top strengths is "input." While I don't *love* negative feedback, I always feel that the more we know, share, and debrief, the better positioned we'll be to improve. I'd much rather hear criticism in a positive way from a family or team member than negative criticism from someone else. We want the people in the congregation to be blessed and strengthened, so we try to discover what needs to be improved—before *they* have to.

After the debriefing portion of our meeting, we often take a quick, five-minute break and then resume, ready to wrestle with the word.

WRESTLING WITH THE WORD

Mike always comes prepared with the word, a golden nugget of truth representing a huge, powerful challenge. Mike's word may come to us complete with three points and several additional Scriptures, but not necessarily. Mike simply articulates the primitive form of the upcoming message in the best way he can. We all take notes.

After hearing the word and throwing our first responses out on the table, the wrestling begins in earnest. We ask ourselves, "So what? How does this message grab me? Where do I have it already 'nailed' in my life, and where do I still need help? What is my 'felt need' as it pertains to this information? Where are the felt needs of the people whom we know and love and with whom we desire to connect?"

DETERMINING THE FELT NEED

At Ginghamsburg, I've learned to celebrate being fully human. I know I don't have all the answers, so I try to "stay in touch enough with my 'earthly mindedness' that I can still be of some heavenly good" (to misquote a popular phrase). Each week in our meetings we ask ourselves, "What is the human baggage we bring to this divine message?" It's a great question to ask yourself when you're preparing a teaching of any kind.

As we discuss the felt need, we won't all agree all the time. Certainly if four thousand people come together for worship (as they do at Ginghamsburg's weekend celebrations), there will be four thousand nuances of felt need represented. But we can no longer get away with pretending that people are dying to hear anything we choose to say just because we're the ones who say it. People no longer attend church out of loyalty or tradition. If people are willing to give us (and God) one hour of their precious weekend time, we need to do everything possible to connect with them. In other words, this had better be good, and it had better be relevant.

Even if it seems as if we'll never agree, we keep wrestling until we've settled on a felt need that will draw people in. No matter how long it takes. We can't cheat or borrow from the time we spend dialoguing with the speaker,

After hearing the word and throwing our first responses out on the table, the wrestling begins in earnest. We ask ourselves, "So what? How does this message grab me? Where do I have it already 'nailed' in my life, and where do I still need help? What is my 'felt need' as it pertains to this information? Where are the felt needs of the people whom we know and love and with whom we desire to connect?"

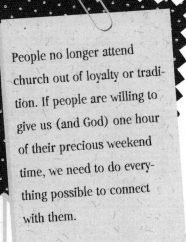

People no longer attend church out of loyalty or tradition. If people are willing to give us (and God) one hour of their precious weekend time, we need to do everything possible to connect with them.

wrestling with the word, and identifying the felt need. The outcome is too important.

I recently visited an enormous church service in Atlanta. They had screens and lighting that made me salivate. I turned six shades of green as I listened to the quality of the sound system. I understood every word of every song, and *all* the words of every song were displayed on the screen. The folks on the stage all knew their parts.

I spent a lot of time reading my bulletin that hour, partly because it was the size of a small novel and partly because I could easily listen and read at the same time. Why? Because from the get-go, no one had engaged my heart. No one had shown me how the day's message from God might be a message I needed for my life. In fact, the first portion of the worship celebration wasn't even directly connected to the message. It was more like a warm-up act to keep us occupied before the "real deal" (the message itself). This worship service had a detailed agenda and a beautiful atmosphere, yet no felt need had been identified. No one was asking the *why* question: "*Why* do I need this hour?" Or the *how* question: "*How* will God use this hour to transform my life?"

The church has never been terribly adept at identifying the felt needs of the culture and addressing them. The world calls this process *marketing*. Jesus called it being fishers of men. He was good at it, and the church can follow his example. Before Jesus began to teach a crowd of people, he fed them. After their needs were met, they were ready to listen. We can start feeding our people's hearts and minds long before the sermon by considering and addressing their felt needs through songs and silence, prayer and participation, humor and hard questions, drama and digital storytelling.

Back to room 202. After about forty-five minutes, I ask Mike if he's ready to move on, if he's had enough time to dialogue with the team to develop the weekend's message. If he says yes, we move on. If he says no, we ask how we can help further. Most great messages come about through some degree of angst. We identify what God has to offer, we struggle with how to access the possibilities, and then we communicate the powerful truth that ordinary people really can live extraordinary lives, under the influence of an amazing Savior.

NAMING THE ELEMENTS

When we're ready to move on, we organize ourselves around a simple list of elements as we seek to give clarity to the worship celebration.

- ⦿ **Word:** the Scripture passage
- ⦿ **Felt Need:** the human issues we bring to this topic
- ⦿ **Desired Outcome:** the goal the team will strive to achieve in the worship celebration
- ⦿ **Theme:** the title we give to the weekend's message
- ⦿ **Look:** the objects, images, processes, or experiences that support the message visually

After the *word* and *felt need* are established, we determine what we want to accomplish through this worship celebration. What is our *desired outcome* for the weekend? How exactly do we hope that people will respond? Will they pray a prayer of salvation? Decide to join a cell group? Open themselves to God's love? Writing down and clarifying outcomes together is a worthwhile exercise. We won't know if we got there unless we knew where we were going in the first place!

Next are the *theme* and the *look*. It's impossible to say which must be designed first, for we can't really control this part of the creative process. We simply begin speaking out and writing ideas and pictures, certain that all will be dreamed and decided upon in time. The *look* is potentially the most difficult element to come up with. Some weeks it takes a very long time to dream up a great new way to visualize a timeless truth, yet when we persevere and hit on just the right look, the creative energy carries us through the week. We've used motorcycles as an image to represent life's ride of faith; we've used old eight-millimeter film footage to communicate leaving a legacy. Once we've agreed on the look, we use it to create graphics, research stories and songs, and design stage décor that will help the message stick visually with an audience that absorbs messages with all its senses.

Sometimes we spend way too long hammering out the "perfect" theme, but in a sense, the theme is our marketing tool. It goes on our Web site. It is displayed on the screen, in the bulletin, in the message CDs, and in the message notes. It is ingrained into our congregation's brains, and that's why we work so hard on creating it. It's like naming a child—except that six people need to agree instead of two!

As we work on the theme, we know that it must be short and quickly

resurrection
alive again

understood. If we have any concern that people may not get it right away, we add a tag line for clarification. Our themes never describe the negative side of the message, always the positive, because Ginghamsburg's brand statement is *where God grows hope one life at a time.* For postmodern people, hope is huge!

Here are some themes and other elements we've used in actual worship celebrations.

- 🎯 ***Word:*** "But God raised him from the dead…because it was impossible for death to keep its hold on him" (Acts 2:24).
- 🎯 ***Felt Need:*** Resurrection is a mind-set that I must first experience.
- 🎯 ***Desired Outcome:*** Participants will stand and move forward in the power of the Resurrection.
- 🎯 ***Theme:*** Resurrection…alive again!
- 🎯 ***Look:*** Butterflies and orange flowers

- 🎯 ***Word:*** "But you received the Spirit of sonship. And by him we cry, 'Abba, Father' " (Romans 8:15).
- 🎯 ***Felt Need:*** I need safety and security…I need the acceptance and care of a heavenly Father.
- 🎯 ***Desired Outcome:*** Participants will embrace and enjoy the love of a perfect Father.
- 🎯 ***Theme:*** Dad Almighty
- 🎯 ***Look:*** Heavenly clouds with a little girl standing in a large hand as in the movie *Bruce Almighty.*

Romans 8:15-16

DadALMIGHTY

- 🎯 ***Word:*** "Do not forget to entertain strangers, for by so doing some people have entertained angels without knowing it" (Hebrews 13:2-3).
- 🎯 ***Felt Need:*** I need to reach out with a deeper brand of Christianity than I'm currently demonstrating.

- *Desired Outcome:* Participants will leave their comfort zones in order to relate to the stranger.
- *Theme:* Strangers Among Us
- *Look:* Human walking down road; shadow is an angel.

DESIGNING THE STRUCTURE

With the elements set in place, we move on to work on the structure of the worship celebration. What music, media, drama, or other multisensory means will we use to communicate these elements in worship? We begin by brainstorming music, whether for the purpose of storytelling, description, or worship. At Ginghamsburg, we embrace an extremely eclectic array of musical choices. Our music director, Fran Wyatt, identifies key words from the message notes and combines his amazing memory with a computer search engine (www.limewire.com is a current favorite) to match them with music selections. The team tries to help and makes a lot of suggestions, but this is Fran's baby. Music selection is Fran's unique gift to the dreaming process, and the songs we eventually end up with must energize and feel right to him.

While Fran is dreaming up music, some of us go to work on media. We may search the Internet for video clips (www.imdb.com, www.visualworship.com, www.hollywoodjesus.com, www.highwayvideo.com, www.avisualplanet.com) or discuss a potential digital storytelling from our own congregation. Our final selections must communicate examples of the message in real-life form. We could shoot an "on the street" kind of intro to the worship service in downtown Dayton, Indianapolis, Columbus, or Cincinnati. (See "What is Your Wildest Life Dream?" on the enclosed DVD.) Or we might choose a real-life scenario that ties in to the message. For example, we used "Jump!" (my own sky diving experience) to represent Zacchaeus' faith commitment to come down out of the tree. (See the video or DVD *The Visual Edge* [Loveland, CO: Group Publishing, Inc., 2001].) Sometimes the media piece takes on a "mission moment" feeling, highlighting an exceptional ministry being carried out by church servants here at Ginghamsburg. The sky and our imaginations are the only limits to what can be done through media.

We also consider various dramatic pieces, including

• reader's theater (a dramatic reading using one or more voices where the players are stationary but expressive),

• dramatic monologues,

• Scriptures read at strategic times, or

• a Bible storytelling woven with an appropriate song selection.

You'll find examples of our dramatic pieces in the Appendix.

As the meeting goes on, we simply let our minds wander as we dream about what could be. "What if…?" we ask. Every week's design team meeting begins as a new canvas, a blank page just begging to be filled with fresh images that convey gospel messages. "What if…?"

And so, eventually, as I keep writing our "brain rain" on the whiteboard, dreams emerge. A design comes through. Thoughts are clarified, and a picture of the weekend's potential begins to form. We're ready to go for it. What have we got to lose?

Jesus said, "Whoever finds his life will lose it, and whoever *loses* his life for my sake will find it" (Matthew 10:39). In our postmodern age, Jesus' words challenge us to lose the performance and replace it with participation, to lose the talking heads and replace them with pictures and stories, to lose the emphasis on numbers of pew-sitters and replace it with numbers of life-losers.

> In our postmodern age, Jesus' words challenge us to lose the performance and replace it with participation, to lose the talking heads and replace them with pictures and stories, to lose the emphasis on numbers of pew-sitters and replace it with numbers of life-losers.

We haven't changed the message here at Ginghamsburg; the message has changed us. Worship celebrations have become the launching pad, the mission control tower for all other ministries. Because even in postmodernity, worship is still the place where the greatest number of real followers check in once a week to refocus, refuel, and refresh their spirits. As the worship team, we're responsible to make sure it happens. But it's never really about us or our ideas.

Worship is the culmination of lives poured out, of real stories told, of the life-changing word being pronounced. God's desire is for us to come, to worship, to change. And so, in this design team meeting, we find agreement in the places we can. We ask for trust from one another in the places that we can't fully agree. We each take our assignments and trust that the Holy Spirit will continue to work in and through us as we leave room 202 and set out to develop the weekend's worship experience.

CHAPTER 6

Developing the Weekly Worship Experience

"Let the beauty

we love

be what we do."

JELALUDDIN RUMI

As the team leader, I make sure that as the team exits room 202, we each have a clear picture of what we are responsible for. Whatever joking and lighthearted fun has transpired in the design meeting, we know that we can count on one another to bring back our pieces of the puzzle on Saturday. You can't serve on this team and not come through. Mike once told me an that organism will reject a foreign virus. You can't function on this team if you need someone to hold your hand…period.

By Saturday evening, we will all be ready. In the meantime, it's my job to keep everyone cohesive. I'll also be writing dramas or other connecting pieces, recruiting stage talent or ministry personnel as needed, and overseeing the design and execution of any required stage and worship area enhancement. All week long I'm in dialogue with team members, checking and double-checking to ensure that we've delivered all the promised pieces with grace and clarity.

As for everyone else…Mike will have a completed message by noon on Friday. Todd will have storyboarded, shot, edited, and produced a classy video, scripted sermon graphic cues, and empowered the unpaid weekend technical team. Brent will have created, critiqued, and re-created the main weekend graphic, the sermon graphics, the song graphics, and the weekend update graphics. Fran will have arranged and rearranged, rehearsed, and restored the weekend's music.

A WEEK IN THE LIFE OF THE TEAM

Because our worship pieces are all unique, no two weekly processes are ever identical. Each of the team players considers his or her work to be art, and art is not necessarily a structured endeavor. We add a little here, take away something there. We tweak, seek counsel, and tweak some more. It's a very intuitive process, but it works because we constantly stay in touch with one another, with the weekly word, and with the felt need we've agreed upon. That's how we can reconvene on the weekend and integrate these individual pieces into one powerful worship experience.

WELCOME TO WEDNESDAYS

While it's difficult to nail down the *specifics* of what the team does throughout the week, it is possible to describe the *types* of tasks we do day to day. In Chapter 5, I outlined the anatomy of the Wednesday design team meeting. Our worship planning always begins on Wednesdays, but it doesn't end there. We may need to touch base with one another, confirming, "Now, we did say we wanted to use warm sepia tones in the main graphic this week, right?" or "Are we sure we'll have a guest saxophone player stage right?" Once we leave room 202, reality sinks in, and we may find ourselves with questions we hadn't thought of before. To make sure we all stay on the same page, someone always carefully copies the "plans" off the whiteboard. By workday's end Wednesday, the plans have been typed into a rough-draft "script."

Wednesdays are also for thinking through who else might be needed for this worship experience. Because we plan so close to the weekend, we must contact any additional personnel by Wednesday night in order to have the best chance at securing their services. If Todd has a video story to produce, he'll be attempting to reach the people he needs for the shoot ASAP to schedule the best time for that to happen. The same goes for any dramatic or musical talent needed.

As we contact these people, we recognize that we may be putting them in a tight spot. For us, timing is critical. Although we try to be as flexible as we can, they may need to change their schedules if they want to participate. Sometimes an explanation about how we work "in the week" helps them weigh the benefits of participating against the realities of their schedules. If they have experienced our worship, they usually understand and appreciate the benefits of in-the-moment ministry. (Our worship teachings and themes are known for being very life-relevant—right here, right now!) Most of the time we figure out a way to make it work.

Ideally, by 6 p.m. Wednesday, Fran has made contact with musicians to let them know who will be needed to perform the weekend music selections. Drama players have been contacted and secured, visual components for the main graphic have been found, and a video shoot has been scheduled. (Key word here: *ideally*!)

Each team member has a good idea of what must be accomplished each day in order to be ready when the weekend rolls around. We all have our daily and weekly to-do lists, which you'll find outlined at the end of this chapter. Once we feel we have a good grip on the worship celebration, we blend into congregational life at Ginghamsburg by giving our gifts and time to other ministry endeavors.

Wednesday night is a huge discipleship class night at Ginghamsburg. Each week we set up tables and chairs to transform our worship area into a "food court" with a full menu. The worship team simply makes sure that the ambience is right. This year (wearing my creative-director hat) I suggested that we go international and let each week represent a different nationality or culture. Mexican night, German night, soul food night...you get the idea. Brent creates a screen graphic to represent that country—a potato with the Irish flag in the background for Irish night, for example. We seek out and play CDs with culturally appropriate background music. Brent also creates graphics for some of the larger Wednesday night classes, and Todd may provide videos from our archives for those learning opportunities.

The food court offers a convenient way for church members to feed their families for a modest price and, perhaps more importantly, encourages them to bring their families to classes. The worship team enjoys the fellowship with the larger body. After eating at the food court with my family, I'm usually off to the public library, on the Internet doing research, or getting ahead on my writing, particularly if a drama is to take place that weekend.

Mike does not usually work further on the message Wednesday. Instead, his day is spent connecting with other ministry leaders or taking care of various responsibilities. He may be teaching a class or simply mingling in the food court to touch base with our people.

> Once we feel we have a good grip on the worship celebration, we blend into congregational life at Ginghamsburg by giving our gifts and time to other ministry endeavors.

THANKFUL FOR THURSDAYS

Thursday is a long day for us, but it's a great work day. Staff chapel at 11 a.m. is the only mandatory meeting. After that, we're free to work as needed on worship pieces. Todd will be working on the video shoot—on the Ginghamsburg campus in a makeshift studio, or potentially as far away as a Hard Rock Cafe in Indianapolis. He may need to take someone along to help or to host the video, but he tries not to tie up too much staff time. When he finishes shooting, he'll come back and begin the long, arduous process of capturing and storyboarding his video, a twenty-five-hour process (average time) that requires artistic thought, concentration, and perseverance. Todd may work until 7 or 8 p.m. at the church, then take his laptop home to do more editing Thursday night.

Brent will be creating and tweaking a main graphic, and sometimes creating an "animation loop" as well. Themes like "We Danced Anyway" may call for a moving graphic, so creating an animation loop is another process that we must incorporate from time to time. In between worship team tasks, Brent is also making time to take on more artistic responsibility for the Ginghamsburg Web site. In addition, he's currently translating our graphics into German to enable a partner ministry in Germany to further kingdom work in Europe and beyond!

Fran is Mr. Arranger on Thursdays. Thanks to Fran's arranging skills, we haven't had to purchase written music in years. Fran charts or writes out all of our music selections using Finale software by Coda Music. His arrangements allow us to inject the Ginghamsburg flavor into any given piece. On Thursdays Fran may have lunch with a ministry person or stop by my office and talk about how things are going in the music ministry. We discuss new plans and ideas and try to solve new problems as they come up. We try to check in regularly in order to maximize Fran's work and ministry potential. Everyone needs strategic partnerships.

By 6:30 p.m. Thursday, the musicians for the weekend have arrived, as well as the "Bridge," our vocal ensemble for worship. They have a preliminary rehearsal, going over the high points so that musicians can effectively practice on their own before coming back together on Saturday. By the time of this printing, Thursday night will officially be "arts night" at the Ginghamsburg main campus building. This will allow multiple music groups, bands, and choirs to rehearse without worrying that their sound might disrupt discipleship classes, which will be scheduled for other buildings or times.

My Thursdays are extremely full. I co-lead staff chapel, connecting the weekend's message to the staff DNA and creating a teaching out of that combination each week. In addition, I try to make myself available as an on-call "creative resource partner" to our staff, especially to the worship and senior management teams. In this role, I might be meeting with our Hispanic contingency to plan their next step in worship connection, interacting with an environment team to talk through our next remodel project, strategizing with a communications team player about a marketing piece, or meeting with Mike to go over the first draft of his message. The tasks change from week to week, but there is always a lot to do as we plan new ministry together.

Thursday evenings I lead a children's choir. This is strategic for me because (1) the kids love it and (2) it brings their parents into the worship celebrations. One of our best-attended weekends of the year happened several weeks ago when our "Kidz on da' Rock" ministered in the weekend worship celebrations. It's exciting to see more people engaged in the worship this way, and everyone loves hearing the kids sing. I co-lead this group with a children's ministry staff person who takes care of the administrative and classroom management details that arise with a sixty-voice children's group. Noel's gifts combine with mine to form another strategic partnership!

After rehearsal, I go home to finish scripting and writing for the weekend celebration. I try to think through every single detail, from the setup to the colors to the worship song graphics to the announcement details. Thursday nights are late nights, but so important for me in completing the worship design process. When I take the time on Thursday evenings to think and write through absolutely everything, Fridays go a lot better. Even in the best weeks, however, final details come together in the slightly chaotic atmosphere of…

FREAKY FRIDAYS

Fridays are chaotic and crazy in most organizations, but I really do love our "freaky Fridays." Rather than just designing our individual worship pieces, we're beginning to share our designs with one another, and I'm growing more excited at what I see and hear. I find myself *humming* the music that Fran is rehearsing. I *like* the weekend graphic and begin to see stage enhancement possibilities for pulling the look together. Mike's message is starting to excite me, and I *like* the written prayer that will lead into it. The freakiness comes in the chaotic busyness of bulletins being completed, weekend classes being prepared, equipment being set up, stages being set, food being cooked, and messages being completed. I love working in this atmosphere of excitement and urgency. Something good is about to happen here!

On Friday, Todd will still be doing major work on the video pieces for the weekend. But he will have connected (via e-mail) with his unpaid weekend crew and checked that everyone has what they need for media success. If we've decided to use a video clip from a movie, Todd and I will verify the start and stop places, and he'll get that ready for the worship celebration. He takes a break from the video work for "micro-team," when he, Brent, Mike, and I gather to hear Mike's finished message.

> The church has traditionally underestimated the power of the human brain to absorb messages through visual imagery.

This core team-within-a-team gathers in Mike's office late each Friday morning, after Mike has finished his message. Just as in our Wednesday design team meetings, micro-team meetings are a combination of lighthearted fun, safe space for challenging issues, and the nitty-gritty of dreaming the imagery that will best enhance the weekend's message. (You can check out our message graphics on the Ginghamsburg Web site, www.ginghamsburg.org.)

Much thought goes into making these visual communication pieces clear, engaging, and original. The church has traditionally underestimated the power of the human brain to absorb messages through visual imagery, and I like to think we're addressing that deficit as we talk through these important pieces. The four of us know each one's best gift to the process, and it's a dialogue that I look forward to each week. Todd is taking Mike's script and creating a new media script just for the message, with in-cues and out-cues for the graphics. Later today he'll type it up and distribute it to his media servants for tomorrow's message run-through. Brent makes a list for his own use, carefully marking which portions of Scripture Mike needs, which version of the Bible he'll be using, and the exact wording of the points to be displayed on the screen.

Brent arrives a little later on Fridays, as he'll more than likely be working past midnight on the graphics for the weekend. He's always anxious to gather for micro-team so that he can get started on his biggest assignment of the week, those message graphics. After micro-team, it's easy to find Brent. He's glued to his computer, and if he goes home, he's glued to his laptop at home until the wee hours of the morning.

Fran spends Fridays attending to details stemming from the long day before. He finishes up arrangements, possibly creating some music or click tracks to program into a sequencer to enhance a special piece. He meets with various other staffers or music ministry servants. He also tries to squeeze in some downtime with his family. Saturdays and Sundays will be a physical and emotional marathon for Fran, so he takes it easy on Friday and works more on Monday than the rest of the team. We don't require Fran to join us for micro-team, but he and I go over the worship script in detail. I may involve him with some of the connection pieces, ask for the vocalists to read Scripture, check and see if he is happy with the transitions as they're written on the script, and verify his final worship song selections. Once we're sure about the worship songs, we create artistic text graphics for the screen, as well as large-print hard-copy versions for the visually impaired.

After micro-team, Mike remains available to address questions about anything pertaining to worship. (All of our offices except Fran's are in close proximity to one another—by my request—so that we have an ongoing worship dialogue pretty much whenever needed.) Mike's Friday afternoons are open for necessary appointments and time with other staff. He may take off early to prepare himself physically for the long weekend ahead, a total speaking time of nearly three hours on his feet.

My Friday tasks are varied and vast. I must come in on Friday morning with a clear head for the upcoming weekend. I must bring in the scripts I've written for our administrative support person to type. After I've proofed, changed, re-proofed, and finalized them, copies are distributed to all the weekend teams: music, media, guest services, deaf ministry, and security. This script becomes our guide for the weekend, allowing the details in my mind to be effectively translated to address the needs of each team.

In addition to the main script, I also write up a checklist for our campus site team, the custodians who will assist me in setting up the physical environment that will create the desired worship ambience. Since our stage, our seating, our balcony spaces, and our technical equipment are movable, I must think through each worship service and specify the exact physical setup that it requires. Different setups are required for different weekends—there is no default. So it's imperative that we're clear on Friday about what we'll need Saturday and Sunday. I write everything down on a checklist (from candles to communion tables), and the campus site team initials each item it has set up. (In the early days I did a lot more of the script typing and physical worship setup myself, and

> Different setups are required for different weekends—there is no default. So it's imperative that we're clear on Friday about what we'll need Saturday and Sunday.

you may have to as well!) Although they don't participate in the advance planning and dreaming stages, I view the administrative assistant and custodial staff as part of the team. It takes all of us to pull this off, and I appreciate them a lot!

After micro-team, I do a final check on the main graphic for the weekend. I give an outline of the message to a graphic artist for the bulletin as well as to our Hispanic translators for Spanish-speaking guests. I devise a call to worship and an additional "@the_source" poll question to be posted on our Web site that day, to be viewed by anyone who might be logging on to peruse the upcoming weekend message.

Other Friday tasks may include rehearsing a drama, deciding the gel color for the ambient lighting in the worship area (see Chapter 10, "Styling the Stage"), checking in with guest services to discover what will be going on in the lobby that weekend, and tracking Todd's progress on the video piece. I love the variety that Fridays represent, yet by 5:30 I am ready for date night with my husband! I'm ready to do something fun and unrelated to worship, to rest and rejuvenate in preparation for the weekend ahead.

SATURDAY INSANITY

Saturday starts out slow but gains momentum as we move toward worship time. In the morning, the media guys may be putting the finishing touches on videos or graphics. Musicians may be rehearsing alone. Fran may be putting some finishing touches on an arrangement or setting up extra musical equipment. I often spend Saturday mornings gathering stage pieces from my own home, a nearby shop, or a hardware store. No matter where I am, I am mentally rehearsing the worship experience to think through how the music will sound, how the stage will look, and how the transitions will feel. If I'm serving as worship host that weekend, I'll be going over my words and searching for the best ways to connect all the pieces.

We all try to come in prepared for the work ahead. By the time I arrive at 1:30, the media and music personnel are already setting up cameras, checking cables and monitors, finishing up the media pieces and rehearsing the band. I take an hour and finish styling the stage with the help of various unpaid servants. I call it Saturday Insanity because we're all excited but nervous. There's always a hint of anxiety in the air because we know we're not quite ready. But ready or not, we hope and expect powerful results from our work. Humor and laughter help ease our fears as teams interact and touch base.

At 3 p.m. Mike, Brent, Todd, and the weekend (unpaid) director gather around Brent's computer to do a message run-through. With scripts in hand, Mike talks us through his message while Brent advances through the graphics program on his computer. Mike makes sure that his thoughts are well-articulated and that his transitions are smooth. Brent makes sure he has all the Scriptures right and that the graphics are pleasing to the team. Todd and the weekend director go over the media script to double-check the in-cues and out-cues for graphics, videos, and cameras. I proof all graphics (including song text and announcements) and listen to Mike's content as well. I ask questions and make suggestions as needed. It's our final team huddle to verify that we have what we need. Meanwhile, down in the worship area, the band is in full swing, rehearsing all the music to make it feel just right.

> There's always a hint of anxiety in the air because we know we're not quite ready. But ready or not, we hope and expect powerful results from our work.

By 3:45 all those involved in the worship celebration (except Mike) are in the worship area and ready for tech rehearsal. (Mike retreats to his office to pray and prepare.) Servants take their places. Cameras are white-balanced and focused. Microphones are checked. Lights are set, and we're off and running. We run through the music, media, spoken pieces, dramatic sketches, prayers, and whatever else needs to happen. We rehearse everything (except the message) in consecutive order and intentionally work to integrate the pieces, as I'll describe further in Chapter 13.

We work hard to maximize our efforts while trying to stay cool, calm, and spiritually collected. In the midst of this intense environment, we've had everything from tornado warnings to vocalist meltdowns on Saturday afternoons. Stuff happens, and it's helpful to enlist support people to take care of other needs (building, maintenance, unexpected guests, and power outages) so that the worship teams can continue their preparation. Taking the time to pray with our various teams is also essential to help ease the insanity and create the environment that will become our worship space.

By 4:30 on Saturday the worship teams are off the stage, the candles are lit, the lighting in the worship area is just right, and a carefully chosen CD is being played over the sound system. The ambience invites worshippers in as the team leaders huddle in an upstairs office to talk and pray through the celebration one last time. Dinner is available at a modest price for those who have been working or rehearsing all day. The meal is prepared in the kitchen by unpaid servants (scheduled monthly) who've found they can best love God by cooking for others.

At five o'clock something magical happens. The moment the band strikes the first chord of the opening music, my insanity begins to dissolve. I realize we can't go back and rehearse again. We're here, opening ourselves in worship, and to a certain extent, whatever happens, happens. While part of me still cares very much about the people's experience and how well the service is going, I confess that the other part gets caught up in worship. I enjoy the team's creation and marvel at the ways the ordinary has intersected with the Divine. It's a miracle.

After the 5:00 service ends, we take a few deep breaths and go into the 6:15 celebration. Following the 6:15 celebration, the team leaders once again huddle in a back room to ask ourselves the hard questions: How did we do? Where did we hook people? Did we distract anyone? Is the music connecting? Is the message working? Did the video inspire us? Small changes are discussed, and refinements for Sunday may be in order. Mike may distill a part of his message to make it more succinct. Fran may have to give a difficult solo to a different vocalist. I may have to change lines in a drama to increase the impact. We try to do whatever it takes to lead worshippers into a powerful God experience.

Home by 8:00—the night is yet young! We all go our separate ways to rest and refuel for...

SUNDAY SERENITY

By 8 a.m. Sunday, the teams are back in place. As servants, we have all parked in the spaces farthest from the building since we'll be here all morning long. Once inside, the coffee is hot, and the smiles are big. The cameras are focusing; the projector is humming. The sound system is up, and the vocalists are in place, warming up for a long morning. Mics are rechecked, and candles are relit. The tweaking is done, and now our morning's task is to take this hour-long experience and make it fresh for each congregation (at 9:00, 10:15, and 11:30 a.m.). At 8:30 we huddle for prayer once more, then head to the worship area for the 9:00 celebration.

As we work our way through the morning, we gain confidence. We find ourselves enjoying the moments with one another, with our people, and most of all with the God who's promised to join us if only two or more will gather in God's name. The pressure of the unknown is behind us now, and we're all doing what we love to do, whether it's pointing a camera, dialing in at the soundboard, speaking into a microphone, or playing a mean bass...*here we are to worship!*

WEEKLY TO-DO LIST
Speaker

❏ Spend time with God early in the week to determine the word and direction for the message.

❏ Attend the weekly worship design team meeting.

❏ Work on the message, seeking insight and creative help from accountability group or creative director as needed.

❏ Present finished sermon to the micro-team (media personnel, graphic artist, and/or creative director) so they can create message graphics.

❏ Set aside time for personal refreshment to prepare and be fully present for weekend worship celebrations.

❏ Deliver "practice message" for team players in order to view completed graphics and make any necessary revisions.

❏ Participate in weekend worship celebrations, including adjusting the message on the spot as needed.

WEEKLY TO-DO LIST
Creative Director

❑ Prepare for and lead the weekly worship design team meeting.

❑ Ensure that each team player has specific, individualized direction and support before leaving the meeting.

❑ Think through potential needs and resources for the upcoming weekend.

❑ Write or oversee the writing and execution of all message-supporting worship components, including the call to worship, prayers, Scriptures, stories, dramas, announcements, and closing words.

❑ Stay in close contact with the speaker to ensure support and cohesion with team plans.

❑ Attend micro-team meeting with the videographer, speaker, and graphic artist to create the message graphics and finalize points for bulletin outline.

❑ Create a program script to clarify order of service, cues, and technical details.

❑ Oversee stage design and floor setup in worship area.

❑ Provide direction to lighting and sound personnel.

❑ Set aside time for personal refreshment to prepare and be fully present for weekend worship celebrations.

❑ Participate in practice message run-through session to ensure the grammatic and artistic quality of all graphics. Provide coaching to the speaker as requested.

❑ Participate in all weekend worship celebrations according to areas of giftedness.

WEEKLY TO-DO LIST
Band Director

❏ Obtain worship themes or Scriptures in advance in order to bring song suggestions to the worship design team meeting.

❏ Ensure that the weekend musicians are in place.

❏ Attend the weekly worship design team meeting.

❏ Oversee the preparation and arrangement of any music needed by band or vocalists.

❏ Connect with other ministry or music teams as needed to extend the music ministry beyond the worship services.

❏ Meet with the creative director to discuss any changes or additions to the weekend worship script.

❏ Confirm worship rehearsal times and plans with audio personnel.

❏ Prepare for and direct initial worship rehearsal.

❏ Double-check that all personnel, equipment, instruments, and support required for weekend worship are in place.

❏ Set aside time for personal refreshment to prepare and be fully present for weekend worship celebrations.

❏ Direct preworship music and tech rehearsal with other worship teams (drama, media, sound, lighting, and so on).

❏ Lead entire music ministry in all weekend worship celebrations.

WEEKLY TO-DO LIST
Videographer

❑ Prepare for upcoming weekend by assuring that all unpaid servants, equipment, and software supplies are secured.

❑ Connect with creative director regarding upcoming themes to best prepare and generate ideas for design team meeting.

❑ Attend the weekly worship design team meeting. Assist team in researching video clips, brainstorming new media pieces, and defining a theme and look for the service.

❑ Secure personnel and props for video shoots as needed.

❑ Produce any media pieces planned for the weekend, securing help if necessary.

❑ Stay in close contact with graphic artist and creative director to ensure a unified visual look for all media pieces.

❑ Attend micro-team meeting with graphic artist, speaker, and creative director to create message graphics. Write cue script for agreed-upon message graphics.

❑ Finish production work. Double-check finished video pieces for correct sound balance and cohesion with weekend look and "feel." Determine the best way to introduce and exit video pieces.

❑ Set aside time for personal refreshment to prepare and be fully present for weekend worship celebrations.

❑ Set up technical equipment in worship area, and work with team to prepare all equipment and personnel for worship.

❑ Lead tech rehearsal for all music, drama, and media personnel.

❑ Participate in practice message run-through session to preview message graphics and video pieces.

❑ Floor-direct all weekend worship celebrations.

❑ As time allows, train and develop new and existing media team personnel.

WEEKLY TO-DO LIST
Graphic Artist

- ❏ Attend the weekly worship design team meeting. Give particular attention to the theme and visual elements of the message.

- ❏ Gain team input on the "look" of the main graphic before leaving the worship design meeting.

- ❏ Gather software, photographs, and other materials necessary to create the main weekend worship graphic.

- ❏ Create one or two mock-ups of graphic. Consult with videographer and/or creative director before finalizing.

- ❏ Attend the micro-team meeting with the videographer, speaker, and creative director.

- ❏ Listen to the message and create a list of graphics to be designed specifically for the message.

- ❏ Meet with creative director to assess additional weekly worship graphic needs (for announcements, worship song words, prayers [if needed], storytelling enhancements).

- ❏ Artistically create all agreed-upon weekly graphics as well as additional special graphics as needed (holiday, baptism, communion, special photos, and so on).

- ❏ Participate in practice message run-through session by displaying prepared graphics as the speaker delivers the message. Refine or replace graphics as needed.

- ❏ Serve on media team as needed during all weekend worship celebrations.

CHAPTER 7

The Teams Surrounding the Team: Working in Community

"Now the body is not made up of one part but of many."

PAUL (1 CORINTHIANS 12:14)

A t Ginghamsburg, we believe that each person in the church is called to service. For some of us, that service is also our vocation, our paid employment. Others serve faithfully without pay, but with equal effectiveness. To recognize the importance of this service, we refer to these workers as "unpaid servants." We're a large church, so we have many unpaid servants who've "signed on" to be a part of the music, media, or worship enhancement teams. Without them, we couldn't do worship the way we do it.

So far we've explored the job descriptions of the core worship design team players and discussed the ways each one contributes to the dreaming and development stages of worship design. But remember, great teams don't just dream and develop together. They also deploy, and deployment requires a larger team. At Ginghamsburg the larger team is filled out with unpaid servants. Each week some of the development and nearly *all* of the deployment are carried out by unpaid servants who've been engaged in this mission. Here's a little bit about who they are and how they serve.

UNPAID SERVANTS IN MEDIA MINISTRY

Integral to the weekend worship's media ministry are these technical, unpaid team players:

Floor Director: This person is the eyes of the worship area and gives the weekend director that particular perspective. The floor director also helps the team to anticipate changes in the worship order, content, or plans.

Weekend Director: This week's captain of the ship. This person is in charge of deciding what goes on the screen and when.

Technical Director: This person executes the weekend director's commands via the video mixer.

Camera Operators: These four people run the live cameras for image magnification and additional visual communication.

All media team members maintain continuous communication and are connected through the headset miking system.

MEDIA SERVANT PROFILE

Meet Steve Crichton

Steve is a forty-four-year-old husband and dad of three boys, whose day job is as a member of the administrative staff of Mercy Medical Center in Springfield, Ohio. However, for ten hours one weekend a month, Steve dons a headset. With graphic cue script in hand, Steve sets out to do his "Jesus job." As a weekend media director, he's calling out cameras, cues, and shots while an unsuspecting congregation worships and remains "in the God moment." Here's what Steve has to say about how he was recruited and trained, and what this ministry has meant in his life.

> My wife and I relocated to Tipp City about five years ago and were immediately impressed that God was moving in the church and was speaking through Pastor Mike. We loved the music and the way the church welcomed all people regardless of their church background. The use of media blew me away. I never knew church could be this energizing and thought-provoking at the same time. We got the message the Spirit was sending and decided we needed to join the church.
>
> I got involved in the media team by responding to an announcement inviting anyone who might be interested in serving as a weekend camera operator to come to an evening training session. It was there that I met Todd Carter, who introduced me to parts of the worship I had appreciated as a member of the congregation, but never really paid a great deal of

attention to nor understood technically. After a little gentle nudging by the Spirit and a follow-up call from Todd, I agreed to be trained to serve one weekend a month.

My real training started when Michael Brown (then only eleven years old, but already a trained, unpaid servant in media) showed me how to use the camera "for real" at a Wednesday evening Bible class. Michael was confident, and I had to keep a sense of calm because the last thing I wanted to do was to show fear to a young man who wasn't as old as my youngest son. Michael's dad, David, was directing and was patient and instructive through my errors, misjudgments, and downright blunders that first evening, and I was thrilled with my new skills, as crude as they were.

The team all seemed to get along well, and I discovered that they always prayed before each Saturday evening and Sunday morning began. I was constantly impressed with the fact that while mistakes were always pointed out and every effort was made to instruct the person making the mistake about what to do correctly, anger was never an issue. I never left the team feeling bad, but rather left them feeling supported in how to avoid the problem in the future. I joined David's weekend team and got hooked by being able to be part of something that seemed so high-tech and professional, yet dedicated to service.

A few months later (after serving a couple times as a cameraman and spending a little time in the loft, watching David and others direct), Todd suggested I might like to direct a weekend myself. I was scared to death all over again but believed in Todd's faith in me. I was encouraged by all of those with whom I served that this was something I could do if I tried.

I cannot begin to describe how nervous I was that first weekend alone up in the loft, with everyone thinking I was going to actually "direct" something. I prayed more that weekend than I can remember having prayed for a long time. What a blessing that weekend turned out to be! I left the church after the last service on Sunday, floating from a combination of nerves and joy for the service opportunity I had.

I never understood how important serving could be to my faith until I got to be part of the media team. I started to feel like the great big church wasn't so big anymore. I felt like it was my church and that God had truly led me to this place for a reason. I started hearing about how important it was to be considered a servant and not just a volunteer. While there is nothing wrong with volunteering for something, serving gives a sense of belonging and a sense of truly being a part of what God does every week at Ginghamsburg. God doesn't need volunteers; he calls out for servants. Sometimes that means you don't have to go to a foreign country but only be willing to be used at home.

Since getting involved in the media team, my wife and I joined a cell group with other couples, and I started leading a men's cell group in our home that meets weekly for Bible study, fellowship, and prayer. My wife has started serving as a driver for our Clubhouse ministry and started picking up food for the food pantry. I've joined the board of the New Path outreach ministry while she serves at the Gingham Clothesline (used clothing store). I have served at each and every conference Ginghamsburg has held since being part of the media team by scheduling corresponding vacation days as much as a year in advance.

It is truly a blessing to be able to be used as a small part of what God does to reach out to people every weekend. I now look forward to my weekends so much that we schedule family vacations and activities around those weekends as much as possible so I don't have to switch schedules with someone else. I love the team and can't imagine not being part of the worship experience at Ginghamsburg as a servant in some capacity. As an added benefit, my wife and I now feel as if we are connected with a wide variety of people, a community where we can find encouragement and support.

UNPAID SERVANTS IN MUSIC MINISTRY

Music ministry is crucial to any church movement and the faithful, devoted, core team players are absolutely essential. Thankfully, however, this ministry area is a great magnet for unpaid servants who have amazing and anointed musical gifts to share. Periodically, we advertise or announce that we are auditioning vocalists and instrumentalists for our music ministry. It is up to the servant to decide how often he or she wants to be scheduled, as each weekend is a large time commitment. Most serve one or two weekends each month, and in serving they find that the music ministry often becomes their place of relational community.

The key players we regularly schedule in are keyboards, drums, bass, electric and acoustic guitar, and, of course, vocalists. But I don't know of any instrument that we'd refuse to use. On various occasions, we've included violin, saxophone, double bass, and even a rain stick. Change-ups are good!

MUSIC SERVANT PROFILE

Meet Keith Hitt

Keith Hitt was a Southern Baptist pastor who, through some major life challenges, lost his wife, his son, and his pastorate all within a few months' time. Over time God has restored to Keith "what the locusts destroyed." Keith is now remarried, has two beautiful sons, and uses our band's drum kit as his new pulpit. Keith is a powerful, passionate part of our music ministry, but don't take my word for it—here's Keith.

My family and I came to a Christmas Eve service at Ginghamsburg, and we were simply "hooked." The tasteful use of contemporary music and media and the casual and inviting atmosphere created by the Ginghamsburg family all made for an unforgettable experience. Shortly after that time, I sensed the Lord leading me to join the mission of Ginghamsburg in order that I might learn as much as I could about this special place.

It wasn't long before I got involved in the music ministry. In the bulletin one Sunday, there was a call for anyone who would be interested in playing the drums in the band. I thought that this would be an excellent way to learn how the worship experiences were planned, prepared, and executed each week—and as a bonus I'd get to play the drums as well!

I began playing in August of 1996, but my "Jesus job" is so much bigger than just playing the drums. While I count it an awesome privilege to be a part of a community of committed servants who make the music that is so vital to the worship experience at Ginghamsburg, the most significant part of my Jesus job is the role I play within the music ministry community. The passion of my heart and the calling of God in my life are fulfilled through my responsibility of leading a Bible study for the music ministry participants on Sunday morning. As we study God's Word in an atmosphere of safety and security, we have the opportunity to share with one another the challenges that life brings to us, and we encourage one another to apply God's teachings to our lives today. Along with time spent in Bible study, our community takes precious time to lift one another up in

*prayer. As we share the burdens of our hearts in this fellowship, God then
uses this community to meet needs and touch lives in the name of Jesus.*

*Making beautiful music for my Lord Jesus is an awesome experience, but
that alone would not be enough to sustain my commitment to Ginghamsburg. I am committed to the experience of making music to God's glory
with a band of brothers and sisters in Christ who are growing together in
the study of God's Word, and providing genuine care and concern for my
family and me. All of these gifts together have provided the assurance
that I am serving in the place that God has chosen especially for me.*

UNPAID SERVANTS IN OTHER WORSHIP AREAS

Remember, part of Ginghamsburg's mission statement is "to serve out of
our Call and giftedness." Our church leadership truly affirms serving and giving as genuine acts of worship. In support of this affirmation, each year we
compile a "Servant Role Catalog" that describes hundreds of unpaid servant
positions, much like a user-friendly classified employment section. (See
http://www.ginghamsburg.org/ministry/serve.php.) Each church participant
is challenged to fill out a servant form through an annual late-summer
"Servant Series" of messages. Team leaders follow up with respondents
quickly and train them well with evening or Saturday training sessions. These
are hands-on opportunities to learn the jobs. We start each servant out with a
limited amount of responsibility. As he or she demonstrates competence, we
increase the responsibility so that each one can be deployed effectively "on
mission." (See http://ginghamsburg.org/sermon and view Mike's "On
Mission" sermon, delivered August 2-3, 2003.)

While the music and media teams are large and extremely important to
each week's celebrations, various other artists and collaborators also participate as servants in the weekly worship experience. When you count them all
up, it's a lot of people to keep connected! I knew these additional worship
contributors didn't necessarily need to meet on a weekly basis, but I wanted
to stay in touch with them. So I began to pull together lists of people who
had responded to an ad in the bulletin or our Servant Role Catalog, people
wanting to serve out of their call and giftedness. With the help of my computer, I can communicate with these people through my e-mail address book.
The address book contact folders are organized according to gifts and areas
of desired service. Here are some examples:

• Actors On Call—experienced dramatic players of all ages who are willing to work within the challenges of our quick turnaround times.

• Artists Anonymous—artistic talents in all mediums: chalk, watercolor, interior design, ceramics, graphic design, and others.

• Photographers—experienced photographers who are willing to use their own time and equipment to capture images for screen graphics or building décor.

• Researchers—"information junkies" who, when given the weekend theme, will send back great quotes and factoids that I in turn share with the speaker.

Besides enriching the worship experience, the additional media elements we incorporate into our worship celebrations create more opportunities to serve. Many people want to help, and now we have meaningful tasks to offer them. There's so much to do! One key role has been filled beautifully by a servant we've come to know as "Resurrection Mike."

Mike Martindale had an amazing recovery from a tragic accident at age sixteen (fourteen years ago). Please watch his out-of-the-tomb story on the included DVD. Most weekends Mike makes himself available as assistant to the entire worship team. There are always candles to be lit, water bottles to be fetched, cameras to be white-balanced, coffee to be secured. Mike is always standing by, ready to complete these tasks and myriad others. Truth be known, we couldn't do worship without Mike. Even if we could, we wouldn't want to. He's the worship cheerleader who passionately encourages us with his words and energy. Every church needs at least one Mike. His pay is the relationships we share and the meaning his servant role gives him.

I could tell story after story. There are so many ways to serve in a worship celebration that is multisensory, multimedia, and multicultural. And worship celebration is only the beginning—only one way for servants to pursue their callings. At Ginghamsburg (and I'm sure in your church, too) other ministry areas offer incredible opportunities for service. People can serve as members of the medic team, as teen dance club servants, coffee shop servers, or prayer counselors. Check out the possibilities at Ginghamsburg's Web site and then begin dreaming about your own. Worship team leaders have a unique and important role in guiding the church's worship, but it's the authentic community who, in the end, create powerful God experiences. It's incredible what God can do through passionate people!

PART THREE:

Nobody Told Me the Road Would Be Easy

"Most people are more comfortable with old problems than with new solutions."
ANONYMOUS

The road to creating powerful God experiences is never smooth. Like any project worth doing, worship design will always present its share of challenges, obstacles that try to keep us from seeing the promise ahead. At times we may feel like giving up. We may run out of money; we may not have enough help. We may get to a point where we simply feel too tired to continue. But if we keep our eyes fixed on our goal, if we remember that our results will have eternal consequences, if we trust our trials to God in prayer, we will eventually overcome. We have God's word on that.

Ten years of serving in the same ministry area in the same church have taught me a lot about perseverance. I've experienced failure and hardship. I've seen servants come and go. But still I keep working. I suppose I'm too dumb or just too stubborn to let the obstacles stand in my way for long. Somewhere in my heart of hearts, I firmly believe that for every problem, God has a solution—and I'm just crazy enough to want to stick around to find out what it is!

I'd like to share with you some of the obstacles we've encountered as a team and as a church movement, in the hope that you, too, can learn the art of overcoming.

CHAPTER 8

Overcoming Obstacles in Worship Design

"You must do the thing you think you cannot do."

ELEANOR ROOSEVELT

When church leaders attend our conferences, they inevitably want to know "the dirt" about our worship ministry—our greatest obstacles, our mistakes, where we went wrong, and how we corrected ourselves. Perhaps we all just need permission to fall down and scrape our knees, blow off the boo-boos, then get up and try again. Every worship planner needs to know that he or she is not alone. Yes, we all make mistakes, and Ginghamsburg team members are no exception.

> "No test or temptation that comes your way is beyond the course of what others have had to face. All you need to remember is that God will never let you down; he'll never let you be pushed past your limit; he'll always be there to help you come through it" (1 Corinthians 10:13, *The Message*).

CONFLICTS AS A CREATIVE FORCE

Conflict is a part of human life. As individuals, we have conflicting feelings inside ourselves. As groups, we experience conflict between people. All families experience interpersonal conflict from time to time, and creative teams should not be surprised when conflict arises. Verbal conflict can actually be a healthy sign that team members feel free to express what's going on inside them.

Assuming that team players embrace a shared set of values (a team or larger church mission statement, for example), when conflict arises, the players can remind one another of who they are and *whose* they are. We don't have to continually reinvent the wheel when we know who we are and what we're about. New ideas and creative suggestions can be examined through the lens of "Is this really *us*? Will this truly communicate effectively to *our* people?" As teams grow into and through this kind of process, the potential tension over *my* ideas versus *your* ideas can be greatly reduced. Instead, we work together to seek out the *best* ideas based on the unique scenario of any given week.

Negative attitudes can persist, however. As a team, we are learning to name any elephant (challenge or issue) that may be in the room as we meet. We then invite the affected team player to talk through what he or she might be thinking or feeling about the issue. Next, the entire team joins in to listen, care, reflect, and speak words of correction, hope, and healing. Occasionally, as the team leader, I will need to speak with a team member privately about an obvious source of angst. Most times we experience a huge emotional release as the person talks through this challenge. Best of all, we allow God to be bigger in our midst as we're challenged by conflict to grow in honesty and trust. Don't be afraid of team conflict. It can serve as a creative force that propels the team toward a new and deepened relationship.

DRY SPELLS IN WORSHIP DESIGN

No matter what ministry we're involved in, no matter what our day job might be, we all go through dry spells. Designing powerful God experiences week in and week out, fifty-two times a year can be creatively exhausting. It's important to realize we are human vessels housing a supernatural force, and that as human vessels we must take the necessary steps to avoid burnout.

Dry spells in the team setting usually signal dry spells in the individual players' lives. When we allow ourselves to forgo daily personal time with God, a weekly day for re-creation, or a seasonal sabbath (vacation time), we put ourselves in a vulnerable position, susceptible to temptation, negative attitudes, burnout, and dry spells. But if we tend carefully to our life of faith, it's the Holy

Here are some ideas for re-creating yourself:

- Pick up a book with a creative or inspiring theme and get *lost* in it.
- Visit an art gallery.
- Attend a conference that will stretch your ministry paradigm.
- Take a walk in the woods.
- Have a long talk with your spouse or a close friend.
- Sit in a different part of the worship area.
- Play with your children.
- Go see a movie with your team.

Spirit's responsibility to come through with the creative flow, and I've never known God to let us down.

As team leader, I don't spend a lot of time worrying about dry spells. Instead, I tend to my own spiritual life and encourage my team members to tend to theirs. My frequent prayer is for the team to stay passionately and powerfully close to God, and then give ourselves permission to dream big worship dreams on the foundation of that intimate relationship.

OVERCOMING OBSTACLES

When you work together as a team for a long time, you begin to realize that you've collectively learned a *lot* from the school of hard knocks. The following "learnings" have turned into valuable life lessons that we find ourselves applying to other areas of our lives as well.

- Never say no to a good idea.
- Twenty-four hours is *plenty* of turnaround time.
- The speed of the players will adjust to the speed of the leaders.
- You're only leading if people are following.
- Good isn't nearly as much fun as great.
- Never save a great, creative idea for later.
- You can't preach someone else's message.
- Discouragement wastes valuable time.

We've had more than our share of obstacles in worship design and ministry in general, but I am growing to believe that God's power is magnified through those very challenges! Our worst screw-ups are often the launching pads for God's best show-ups! Let me share a few examples.

THE SCENARIO: It's October 2000. As a church, we've just discovered that for postmodern Christians, tithing is no longer an unspoken assumption, and our offerings painfully reveal this discovery. We make a new commitment to teach tithing and generous living in a strategic three-week stewardship series that will culminate in a commitment weekend.

THE OBSTACLE: Postmodern Christians don't know the definition of church words such as *stewardship* and *tithing*. We need to give information and inspiration without intimidation—all in thirty minutes! In addition, the team has decided that it's distasteful to show real, green money on the screen as part of the "main graphic." How do we teach these important lessons in a language that postmodern people can understand and receive?

THE OVERCOMING: We're in our worship design meeting and have gotten as far as *nowhere.* How do we creatively inspire people toward lifestyles of generosity? One person happened to note that the concept of the tithe (10 percent) was most real to us as a culture within the context of the game of Monopoly...

"Oh, you mean where the card says to pay 10 percent income tax?"

"Yeah, that's my only paradigm for the 10 percent rule."

"But that's about taxes, not tithing."

"So...what if...we came up with our *own* game?"

"What? Like Monopoly for Dummies?"

"Well, sort of...but we'd have to make it our *own* and not be condescending."

"We could write a drama script for people playing Monopoly. That way we could also use play money on the screen (in the main graphic) and avoid the stigma of real money!"

"Yeah, and the players could land on certain squares and have to pay a tithe. Then we could explain what a tithe is through the skit dialogue!"

"Oooh...we're getting somewhere. Then people won't feel so out of it, knowing that the lovable guy in the skit didn't know either."

"Now we're really getting somewhere."

"So what do we call it—the game—the weekend, I mean?"

"I don't know; we can't call it 'Monopoly'."

"True. How about 'Generous-opoly'?"

"Generous-opoly...gener...opoly!! *Generopoly!* The Game of Generous Living!!"

"I love it; I love it; I love it!"

"Me, too! I can't wait to write the script!"

> My frequent prayer is for the team to stay passionately and powerfully close to God, and then give ourselves permission to dream big worship dreams on the foundation of that intimate relationship.

We overcame the obstacle of the typical, dry stewardship sermon using language that people do not understand, by giving this celebration our best creative energies. You can read the results in the Appendix. The "Generopoly" skit was terrific, and God showed up! Our annual stewardship series is now a favorite among our people and is never, *ever* boring! Postmodern people are truly "getting it." We are learning to understand how giving is a vital part of radical discipleship. We continue to try to present ancient truths in culturally relevant ways, and God is glorified. Here's another example.

THE SCENARIO: We have traditionally used the Martin Luther King holiday weekend to deliver a message that reaffirms our call to demonstrate a multiracial and multigenerational kingdom community. The significance of this weekend reminds us that God's desire is for all created children to worship and serve together. Often we've invited a dynamic black preacher to deliver this important message that is always well-received.

THE OBSTACLE: On this weekend in 2003, we needed a dynamic speaker but were having trouble finding one. We had thought Mike would be in town and that he could use this message to recast his multicultural vision. As it turned out, Mike had to be out of town.

THE OVERCOMING: God had been working in the life of Francis Wyatt, our music director, and I knew that he had something to say. In addition, Fran

was already part of the design team. He knew what it would take to present a powerful message to several thousand listeners. Most of Fran's real-life experiences growing up as an African American in St. Louis, Missouri, had yet to be told to our mostly white congregation. "Speaking on this weekend could only make Fran's worship-leading ministry more effective," I thought.

And so…Fran agreed to preach that weekend. We filled out the service with gospel songs and quotes from Martin Luther King Jr. The rest of the team rallied around Fran in a huge way. His humble acceptance of our coaching, combined with the remarkable experiences he had to share, enabled him to preach a great message. In the end, Dayton's Channel 22 news featured Ginghamsburg as their top story that night, amazed that a church in Tipp City, Ohio (98 percent white community), would have such a multicultural flavor of worship.

We overcame the obstacle, the absence of a "traditional" preacher, and God showed up in a powerful way. Let's look at a recent example.

THE SCENARIO: It's May 2003. Mike has come excitedly into the design team meeting with a metaphorical story about his sister's cat, once a stray at her door that wouldn't go away. Eventually his sister let the cat in, but only into one room of the house. Ultimately, after much persistence,

"Socks" was allowed free access to the entire house and has since become a beloved house pet.

"Socks is Jesus," Mike relayed. "He's at the door."

"Cool," Todd exclaimed after Mike left the room. "We could give it a Dr. Seuss *Cat in the Hat* look." *The Cat in the Hat*? In church?

THE OBSTACLE: Dr. Seuss is not widely known as a source of *spiritual* inspiration. How would we take such a childish look and make it deeply spiritual? I wasn't sure how we'd accomplish it, but I challenged the team to "trust forward" that we'd figure it out.

THE OVERCOMING: Todd went ahead to Cincinnati to shoot Mike's sister's story, featuring the real Socks. We'd show this video at the beginning of Mike's message. (See the story of Socks on the accompanying DVD.) Brent went to work on graphics with the help of Sarah Gillenwater, a talented freehand artist. I secured a copy of *The Cat in the Hat* from the library and began to dream...

What if we wrote our *own* cat-in-the-hat story so that Jesus shines through somehow? What if I wrote a story instead of a normal call to worship, featuring a young teacher telling the story "Socks Knocks" to real children sitting on real mats on the stage? The grown-ups in worship that weekend could see our re-created Seuss-like illustrations on the screen as the stage storyteller turned the pages of her book.

I've included the resulting story in the Appendix. "Socks Knocks" became one of our most creative, spiritual, *and* appreciated weekends ever. People were touched by the familiarity of the Dr. Seuss look and the simplicity of Jesus' timeless invitation, "Behold, I stand at the door and knock" (Revelation 3:20). (To view "Socks Knocks," go to http://www.ginghamsburg.org/sermon and click on the May 24-25, 2003 sermon link.) Our music leader went on to connect the message to the song celebration by reminding the congregation, "We've come to worship the one who asks to come into our house today, the one who is Savior and Lord."

Rather than miss out on a great culturally familiar metaphor, we overcame the obstacle and instead *connected* the look to the Jesus story...and God showed up! At least a hundred people made first-time decisions to "open the door of their hearts" that weekend. (When was the last time you came forward to an altar and found a swimming goldfish, a black umbrella, and a tall, red-and-white-striped hat, all nicely arranged there?)

WHAT IS IN YOUR HAND?

Obstacles are nothing new. All the biblical "movers and shakers" had them. Our challenge is to move over, around, or directly through them as God leads. At first, Moses saw only obstacles to the mission. When he tried to look ahead, he saw only his own low self-esteem, lack of the right social connections, and fear that the Israelites wouldn't believe that God had sent him.

But God is the ultimate overcomer, who stands poised and ready with resources to help us past the obstacles. In Exodus 4:2, God asks Moses the powerful question: "What is that in *your* hand?" I like that question.

What is in your hand? What is it that *you already have* that is familiar to you? It's your tool of the trade, your long suit, your strength. It's your best thing. What is in your hand? *Play to your strengths.* Just as God turned Moses' familiar walking stick into a powerful snake when Moses threw it down, God wants to take our "best things," the most familiar tools from our hands, and make them more powerful for kingdom use.

I remember one stormy January Sunday morning at Ginghamsburg. Snow had been falling, blowing, and drifting for days. Our county was under a level three snow emergency, yet we were determined to "have church" for anyone who needed hope for their life. (No snow days for us!) The obstacle that day was clear: The storm would keep most of our musicians and media personnel at home, as they lived some distance away.

What was in our hand? Mike was there and excited about delivering a teaching to a smaller group…that's what was in his hand. I could lead worship and play keyboards (not well, but *could,* and that's what was in my hand). Our graphic artist could play guitar in the absence of our regular musicians; that's what was in his hand. We pulled an image of a frost-covered mountain off the Internet to use as "stained-glass window" wallpaper on the screen. We sang, worshipped, prayed, and listened that day to what God wanted to say in the middle of the storm…and God showed up! All God asked us to do was to be faithful with what he'd already put in our hands.

What has God put in your hand? A beautiful old sanctuary? A unique urban setting for your ministry? A powerful storyteller? A donated cappuccino machine that's just begging to supply coffee to seekers in your lobby? Look in your hand, then trust God to work with what you find there. Know you can overcome the obstacles that seem to be in your way. Keep moving forward, and don't be surprised when you discover that God has shown up!

CHAPTER 9

Four Mantras for the Mission

"I thank God for my handicaps, for through them, I have found myself, my work, and my God."

HELEN KELLER

When Jesus walked the earth, I'm sure he had his share of really bad days. Days when his team really didn't "get it." Days when he couldn't get enough time with his Boss. Days when the needs around him exceeded the resources available to do anything about them. Days when he might have wished he could call it quits.

I remember having one of those really bad days myself years ago. The team wasn't "getting it." I couldn't seem to connect adequately with my co-workers, and it seemed that my problems outweighed my solutions ten to one. Mike, knowing of my discouragement, trudged into my office just before leaving for home and blurted out four action steps—created on the spur of the moment just for me. Four "mantras," if you will. I wrote them down on a yellow sticky note. Mike doesn't even remember saying them (which proves his hunch about how much he has in common with Balaam's donkey—he's just an available body for God to speak through!). But that little yellow square has been taped next to my computer ever since that day. Those mantras have guided me out of many dark moments. Hopefully, they'll help you too.

MANTRA 1: Work in the Package God Has Given You

"I praise you because I am fearfully and wonderfully made"—King David (Psalm 139:14a).

How many of us, after returning from a worship conference, find ourselves somewhat inspired yet quietly confused? We've seen how others are doing it. We've observed their talent and the great ways God is using them. We've written down everything the speaker had to say. We've made real decisions to do things *better*. Yet even in the wake of this inspiration, we experience a disconnection. "How am *I* supposed to replicate what they're doing? How is *our* church going to take all the necessary steps to become like *their* church?"

Part of the good news of the gospel is that we don't have to try to be like anyone else. To attempt to replicate another worship leader's persona or ministry would be a slap in the face to the One who has "fearfully and wonderfully" made each one of us. Our creator God has given each one of us a unique package...a soul. Your soul is the unique part of you. Your soul is your personality, your God-given wiring, the you inside...the person you were created to be. *The Message* translates it this way: "Whoever did want him, who believed he was who he claimed and would do what he said, he made to be their true selves, their child-of-God selves" (John 1:12, *The Message*).

> To attempt to replicate another worship leader's persona or ministry would be a slap in the face to the One who has "fearfully and wonderfully" made each one of us.

God-esteem. We need it to thrive. The Bible commands us to love God with all of our mind, strength, heart, and soul (Mark 12:30). We can't love God with our souls (much less teach others to do the same) if we don't know who we are inside. When we strive to become someone else (even someone we admire), it's as if we've disowned our own souls somewhere along the way. We can't become our true selves when we're trying to become someone else.

I need the community around me to keep reminding me of who I am in God. In my moments of discouragement, I've been known to sit myself down in front of my husband or a close friend and say, "Tell me again how God has equipped me for this job...I forget! Tell me again what you see God doing through me." I do forget, and hearing those kindred spirits tell me who I am in God's eyes refreshes me. It restores my soul. I have to like *me* before I can *love* you—Jesus said so: "Love the Lord your God," and "Love your neighbor as yourself" (Matthew 22:38-39). I can't love God or others until I've truly embraced the simple gift of my soul, the unique part of me that God created, loves, and desires to work through.

God has given *you* a package, a soul. It's a gift to use as you live out your dreams. It's your gift to exercise as you design worship experiences that will draw others to know that same kind of grace and acceptance from God.

Once, while designing a worship experience that I hoped would guide participants to truly understand and embrace this amazing-grace kind of love, I rewrote Psalm 23 as though I were speaking it to God in my own words. I asked the members of the congregation to close their eyes as they imagined this intimate interchange with God...

SCRIPT: *The Lord Is My Shepherd*

The Lord is my shepherd—mine, all mine. He remembers to feed me. He presses oil into my wounds. He counts me as his own, for I am important to him. When I'm missing, he comes after me. He won't sleep if I can't. He loves me and I shall not want. There's nothing I could need that he hasn't assessed and blessed on me.

This God makes me lie down in green pastures. And I'm just gonna lay here and stare at the sky and dream. Dream about what can be now that the sky's the limit. Dream about my kids, my family, my friends, and all God will do in their lives…just because I asked and God can.

This God leads me beside still waters. I look down at my reflection—I can see it clearly. I am the son, the daughter, the beloved child of the most-high God…and I like being that person. God has taught me that love.

This God, my shepherd, restores my soul. Perfect? No. Lovable? Yes. Restoration can be appreciated only by the sinful, the broken, the spiritually challenged…the shamed child, the abused teen, the overwhelmed mother or father.

This God restores my soul, picks me up, and leads me on a new path of righteousness, not for my sake or my glory, but for his name's sake. Yes, I will walk through the valley of the shadow of death. We all will, but we will fear no evil. Evil cannot touch us. The shadow of death is simply a shadow—not the real deal. *For you are with me.*

Death, where is your sting? Grave, you have no victory. Jesus the shepherd is here. His rod of fierce protection, his staff of clear direction, they comfort me.

You prepare a table before me in the presence of my enemies. You've written my name on the invitation, you've anointed my head with oil…

You've deemed me forgiven and useful for service. Those who rejected you now watch while you and I eat and laugh and talk together. I keep drinking out of my cup, but it keeps getting refilled to overflowing. You're amazing, God. Surely this God's goodness and mercy—the unconditional, unrelenting, unbridled love of God—shall be with us all of our lives. Every day, if we will only look for it…if our ears will simply listen…if our hearts will readily receive it. And we will live in God's house forever. Amen.

As worship designers, we must work in the package God has given us. How is God best able to use you and your team? What is the language you speak best? Some people are oral communicators, masters of the spoken word. Others say it best with pictures, getting the God story by carefully aiming the camera at the most important thing. Some are careful planners, making each moment count, using people and resources to their full potential. Others gifted in relationship building can communicate by their congregational connectivity. They will be used by God to make others feel welcome and loved.

At Ginghamsburg, one of our most vivid examples of a team member "working within the package" is Francis Wyatt, our music director. When Fran leads worship, he starts out behind the congas and timbales, but he just can't stay there. He walks (or hops) across the stage as he engages the entire congregation in song and worship.

Depending on the tone of the song, you might see Fran standing in the lineup with the lead vocalists, facing the vocal ensemble as a choir director, or standing on the very front edge of the stage to pray with the congregation or lead into the next song. Once Fran, a bit perturbed that the congregation had slipped into "lazy worship," took his drumsticks and flew down off the stage. He circulated through the crowd (a highly interactive worship experience!), encouraging our people to sing out! Back on the stage, the band continued to follow his "sign language." (They can be led from anywhere.) It's an amazing kind of worship leader package that Fran has!

Tom Lipps, the talented keyboardist who occasionally leads in Fran's absence, is a twenty-six-year-old Italian Catholic with a strong Campus Crusade background. When Tom leads, he stays behind the keyboard...three keyboards, in fact. (He can never have enough. We're giving Tom a third "prosthetic" arm for his next birthday.)

Even if Tom were not a keyboardist, you just wouldn't want him doing some crazy dance across the stage. Tom is not a *physical* performer. He is, however, quite an effective and engaging worship leader in his own right. Tom's clear voice, facial expressions, and command over his instrument help guide the congregation into true worship. What a shame it would be for Fran or Tom to try to be more like each other. God has truly given each of them a unique package to work in, and our congregational worship is richer because of their differences.

Each one of us absolutely must work in the package God has given us. We ask our trusted mentors and friends, "When have you experienced God powerfully using me?" While some are best one-on-one, I am better in front of a crowd. While some can paint beautiful pictures with a brush, my best art is in the arrangement of tactile objects. Some people are powerfully gifted vocalists who minister through song. I'm better at interweaving popular songs with biblical storytelling and choosing the right people to sing them. That is my package, and I'm learning to be comfortable in it.

MANTRA 2: Tell the Truth

When Jesus boldly announced, "The truth shall set you free," was he referring to the truth about God, or the truth about everything? Could this statement have been a piece of wisdom that Jesus believed, demonstrated, and lived out every single day of his life? I believe Jesus was stating that the truth, any truth about any given life situation, would ultimately set us free if we could but discover it and speak it.

> Telling the truth to one another in community is nothing short of an art form. We speak the truth in order to build one another up, to give constructive insight into one another's life stories.

Telling the truth to one another in community is nothing short of an art form. We speak the truth in order to build one another up, to give constructive insight into one another's life stories. (This is not an invitation to blanket our co-workers with criticism or announce our personal opinions to the world!) As we tell the truth within our teams, we must be motivated by love. We must hope and intend success for everyone involved. We must join in one desire to enjoy all God's best gifts as a team, a community, and a church.

As the leader of the worship design team, I hold stewardship of the congregation's worship experience. My job is to consistently and continually tell the truth about our worship pieces in order that the pieces might best serve the kingdom. In the best sense of truth telling, this means affirmation whenever possible, and suggestions for improvement when improvement is called for.

I tell Mike the truth about his messages and how they affect me. I tell Fran the truth about his growth as a worship leader, how the music ministered that weekend, and how important his musical contribution is to the overall worship experience. I tell Todd and Brent the truth about where their media pieces shine and where they could connect with people a bit better. I ask the other team players to tell me the truth about pieces I have prepared as well. "Did that connect? What do you think about this storytelling script? How does the stage look to you? Do you think we're on target here?"

Being truthful is imperative for our growth process. I remember a time early on when, as an unpaid servant, I had pulled together and coached a team of four women to execute a drama using a purchased script I'd found in a catalog. These ladies were doing an excellent job of acting. I had created the drama set, and we rehearsed and performed the drama for our Saturday night celebration. Afterward, as we quietly debriefed together, Mike told me the truth as he saw it.

"The drama is good, Kim, but it doesn't really go with the message. There's a disconnection for me. I'd recommend we pull it from tomorrow's worship celebrations." This was devastating news, of course, since we'd obviously put in a significant amount of time and work already. I reluctantly agreed to drop the drama, but in responding I told the truth about my feelings. "I feel bad about that for myself and mostly for the others involved," I replied, "but I'll do the best thing for the church family and the overall worship experience."

I went home, prayed for strength and courage, and then phoned each of the four actors. "You did an awesome job tonight, and I loved working with you," I told each one, "but in the end, the drama did not connect with the sermon the way we'd hoped. It isn't anyone's fault. We would love to use the drama and especially your gifts in the future, but we're going to have to pull it from tomorrow's celebrations."

I told the truth but affirmed each person's contribution. Much to my amazement, not one of them reacted negatively, and each one has had opportunities to serve in dramatic roles since that time. The worship celebrations the next morning were much better. The word was much more powerful without the confusing drama, and God was honored.

In that situation the simple truth set all of us free, and I grew in the process. Here is what I learned that weekend that has stuck with me—freedom lessons I've since used over and over:

• No matter how great a drama is, without a direct connection to the message it cannot play a powerful role in the worship celebration.

• The majority of our dramatic scripts must be original and written by someone who knows and understands the intention of the speaker's message.

• Most people can handle the truth if it's spoken with love and authenticity, affirming the things they've done well.

• The way we react in times of great challenge or seeming opposition reveals our true character.

• Others on the team can trust me with their true feelings.

When I tell the truth, other team members are freed to do the same. And that makes the next mantra a more viable possibility.

MANTRA 3: Do the Right Thing, Not the Expected Thing

Author Anne Lamott wrote, "Hope begins in the dark, the stubborn hope that if you just show up and try to do the right thing, the dawn will come. You wait and watch and work: you don't give up."

Powerful God experiences are not going to just spontaneously descend into your worship space. This is not to say that God won't powerfully "show up" unannounced at various times, but simply that God has always honored the work of those who "wait and watch and work." As worship designers, we must pray, prepare, and persevere in doing the right things rather than taking the easy way out. We may be tempted to take the easy way out in several ways:

• By allowing team players to come and go from the design team meeting as they wish, never bringing focus to the worship design process.

• By using the same tried-and-true worship songs over and over, rather than searching for new possibilities. Remember, God wants us to "sing to him a new song" (Psalm 33:3).

• By saying, "That's not my job," when faced with a task we don't want to take on.

Even as I write this list, I am aware that this mantra permeates everything we do here at Ginghamsburg. (I could probably continue the list until the last page of this book!) This is a piece of our team's DNA that we cannot minimize or overlook. We know we will never make our best decisions unless we set aside our fears of encountering resistance or increasing our own workloads. We recognize that if we try, we may fail. But most of the time we try anyway. If we want our worship dreams to succeed, we know we must wake up every day and do the hard things, the right things.

Most worship designers want to encourage incredible God experiences, but we tend to underestimate all it will take to get there. Thomas Edison said, "Genius is one percent inspiration, ninety-nine percent perspiration." Jesus Christ said, "But small is the gate and narrow the road that leads to life, and only a few find it" (Matthew 7:14). There are no shortcuts in this endeavor. It's a thousand little decisions every single week. When we've chosen to live life on the narrow way, we must work hard to maximize every single moment of the worship experience. Thankfully, Jesus will never leave us alone on the path.

MANTRA 4: Go in God's Authority

"But you will receive power when the Holy Spirit comes on you"
—Luke (Acts 1:8a).

Moses was obviously chosen by God for one of the most monumental leadership tasks of the entire Old Testament. An Israelite by birth, Moses had been raised as an Egyptian. This gave him the perfect "crossover credentials" to succeed in delivering God's chosen people from slavery. The only trouble with Moses was inside Moses himself. He didn't realize how uniquely gifted he was, nor did he recognize the power of God being offered to him in the deal. Moses was full of excuses for why he couldn't pull off the Promised Land proposal.

I've had my own set of excuses. I've even spiritualized them at times…excuses as to why God could use others much more effectively. Here's my "short list" (I'll spare you the long one):

• I'm a female (and grew up in a denomination that refused to recognize females as leadership material).

• I'm a *small* female (easy to be underestimated).

• I didn't pursue a four-year college degree.

• I'm not particularly left-brained, and my right-brained tendencies can be very limiting in certain structured scenarios.

• My dad was mentally ill, creating a dysfunctional childhood environment.

• I'm not ordained clergy.

How's that for starters? How ironic that I would be signed up to serve as creative director, designing worship in a megachurch whose empowerment theology has challenged every one of my excuses! My challenge to go in God's authority has increased as I've occasionally been called on to create powerful God experiences without a "preacher." I've even had to *be* the preacher on occasion.

For me, "Go in God's authority" usually translates as "Feel the fear and do it anyway. God will do the rest." God's question to Moses, "What is that in your hand?" (see Chapter 8) is a question for me as well. God works in me, just as he worked in Moses, to convince me to rely on his authority rather than my own. "In my hand," I know I can count on a passionate band, versatile vocalists, motivated media-savvy partners, and a team who will put up with and build on my wildest worship dreams. Also in my hand is my own creative ability to pull all kinds of diverse, multimedia pieces together to produce a cohesive and powerful message.

As a team, we've had to ask, "What is in our hand?" as we've encountered occasional weekends when we dream, develop, and deploy worship together without the aid of a preacher. We refer to these experiences as "team weeks." On these weeks I come with a word, a theme, and a core truth, and the team then creates a worship experience with music, drama, and media—but no traditional sermon or message.

Our first "team week" fell on a pre-Thanksgiving weekend a few years back. With no traditional message-giver on the schedule, we knew as a team that we'd be the messengers for the weekend—that we must move out and *go in God's authority*. As we met to design the worship service, we agreed on a few key things:

• The bulk of the "message" time could and should be God stories—video or live testimonies of God at work in our people's lives.

• This pre-Thanksgiving worship celebration should not just remind participants to be thankful. Rather, it should encourage them to rejoice *in the midst* of painful situations.

• The celebration must include a word of hope, for "we know that in all things God works for the good of those who love him, who have been called according to his purpose" (Romans 8:28). This Scripture helped give form to our creative work.

We asked some additional staffers to join us in room 202 to help brainstorm a list of the possible God stories we could feature. Some of our favorites came from people inside that room. One staff person's unmarried daughter had just announced an unexpected pregnancy. Several years ago, another staff person's baby had died of complications at just three months of age. A third story would describe the experience of a fifty-something couple, husband and wife, both Ginghamsburg servants, battling the wife's cancer.

As we contemplated the potential of sharing these family stories with the larger congregation, Fran came up with the idea that unlocked our creativity: "We can frame this around the dance of life! 'We Danced Anyway' is a song I've been wanting to do."

Immediately the team knew we were onto something powerful, an alternative Thanksgiving celebration—three stories told about God's faithfulness in the midst of challenging life circumstances. One of these stories (the Ginghamsburg couple battling cancer) can be viewed on our video/DVD resource, *The Visual Edge.* Another story was presented as a live monologue and is included in the worship script provided in the Appendix. You may want to use this script outline and insert stories from your own church community.

We have challenged our congregation to *go in God's authority* by telling their stories to encourage others. It's exciting to see how real people have responded with real stories that become part of God's movement to do real kingdom work. As a church, one of our principles of renewal is the "Priesthood Principle." [1] Simply put, this principle states that God works best through everyday people. Ginghamsburg is not a movement of professional clergy but of everyday, ordinary people, real followers committed to carry out the mission of Jesus on planet Earth. Postmodern worship is a lot about storytelling, and the more people are empowered to *go in God's authority*, the more stories there will be to tell.

On a recent Palm Sunday weekend, we invited a larger group of unpaid servants to join us for a "team week." "In our hand" was a story, the story of Jesus' last week on earth. As a church, we had not chronicled that story together in worship for at least ten years. I began mapping out a musical drama, keeping in mind the strengths of the people who might be part of such an event. As we endeavored to move ahead in God's authority, we were again met by a powerful God experience. Many from our congregation remarked afterward that it was their favorite worship celebration ever. You'll find an outline of that worship experience in the Appendix.

> Postmodern worship is a lot about storytelling, and the more people are empowered to *go in God's authority*, the more stories there will be to tell.

THE MESSAGE OF THE MANTRAS

All four of these mantras have guided me as I've worked with people, projects, and God possibilities. Remembering them has been so very *freeing* as I make daily decisions that will have eternal impact. Now, whether I'm casting roles for a children's musical or designing a special altar for a 9/11 anniversary, I hear God say, "Kim, just work inside of who you are; tell the truth! Do the right thing, not the expected thing. I have given you all authority—for heaven's sake...go!"

When we ignore these four mantras, we find that we have music without passion, media without power, and messages without purpose. I don't know anyone who wants to be part of a mediocre movement. We don't want to meet our Maker only to find out what God *could* have done through our lives, if only we hadn't played it safe and done the comfortable thing rather than risked doing the creative thing.

It's amazing to see what kind of miracles unfold when we *work in the unique packages God has given us*; when we *speak the truth in love;* when we determine to *do what is right, not merely what's expected*; and when we step out and *go in God's authority*. By doing these things, everyday people demonstrate the power of an extraordinary God!

Endnote

1. See Michael Slaughter, *Spiritual Entrepreneurs* (Nashville, TN: Abingdon Press, 1996).

Multisensory worship is worship that engages the senses. People absorb messages better when all their senses are engaged. Rather than just expecting our people to listen to "talking heads," at Ginghamsburg we give visual representation to the message with screen graphics or video and stage displays. We invite worshippers to take the hands of the persons on either side as we go to God in prayer. Communion becomes an opportunity to "taste and see that the Lord is good" (Psalm 34:8) as we serve fresh bread dipped into the cup. Much care is given so that each worshipper feels comfortable and engaged. Jesus knew the value of a well-prepared environment. "I go and prepare a place for you," he told us (John 14:3), and then promised he'd come back to take us there one day soon.

In this section you'll find practical steps and valuable insights to help you incorporate multisensory elements into your worship services. We'll start up front on the platform, then work our way back through the entire worship area. Get ready for some moving and shaking—your worship area may never look quite the same again!

CHAPTER 10

Styling the Stage

"Think left

and think right

and think low and think high.

Oh, the THINKS you can think up if only you try!"

DR. SEUSS, OH, THE THINKS YOU CAN THINK

I come from a long line of furniture rearrangers. My earliest memories are of my mom and her mom sitting in my grandmother's living room, talking through all the possibilities a furnished room could offer. They were always mentally arranging and rearranging things, then they'd share their ideas with each other…

"We could put the piano on that south wall, Marian."

"But where would we put Great-grandma's hutch?"

"Well, it could move around to the wall over next to the window. The light would still flow in real nice."

"I never thought of that! Still, the old secretary would need to go. It's been crowded ever since you brought that old thing out here."

"You're right. I'll ask Daddy to move it back to the bedroom."

"Then you'll have to bring the slipper rocker back out here."

"I suppose I will."

On and on they'd go. It was like therapy for Depression-weary minds. I'd listen intently and try to picture each move they described right along with them. What that gentle banter taught me early on was that things can be rearranged. They can change. Despite our limited financial resources, we're not stuck here with the "same old same-old." We can make the very same room look totally different every single week if we want to. As my colleague Sue Nilson announces upon her arrival at the office each morning, "All-new day, all-new chances!" I truly love the concept that we can change our environment to suit the needs of the occasion.

Imagine my dismay when I first stepped inside a traditional church building and found all the furniture in the sanctuary bolted to the floor! That particular church configuration spoke volumes to my spirit. It said, "We're committed to never changing; we must keep things exactly as they are week after week, year after year." Worshipping communities inhabiting even the most traditionally furnished church buildings are discovering new ways to use old spaces. Whether it's removing some fixtures from the platform, placing media screens in tasteful locations, or adding candles or other sources of warm, ambient light, there is always a way to breathe new life into the worship space.

Postmodern worship is best expressed in pictures and stories in the authentic context of where real people live. "Styling the stage" is simply creating a fresh worship environment where the story, message, and theme of the weekend can be best expressed and lived out.

At Ginghamsburg, this is accomplished through a team effort that includes brainstorming together, drawing in all the factors we can, and continuing to think and dream together as we begin physically creating the environment. Allow me to take you through the various steps of this informal and artistic process.

THE PREPARATION

We are working with a guest speaker this weekend, a delightful young Hispanic woman who, though ordained in her native Mexico, serves an Ohio pastorate close by as a missionary to the United States. Early on I began thinking about how we might take full advantage of this speaker's unique ethnicity, and encouraged the team to pull out their most creative Latin or Mexican-related pieces. In the hallway and lobby areas, we will serve salsa and chips cheerfully arranged on tables featuring chili peppers as décor. In the worship area we'll hear the ambient sounds of Salvador (an excellent Latin-American band) prior to each worship celebration. On the large screen will be a main graphic created to give visual representation to Lupina's message. Here are the elements of the message that Lupina will bring to us:

- ⦿ *Word:* 1 John 4:16-21
- ⦿ *Felt Need:* Emotional pain keeps me from receiving and giving authentic love.
- ⦿ *Desired Outcome:* Participants will receive and begin speaking God's language of love.
- ⦿ *Theme:* Love—the Universal Language
- ⦿ *Look:* A multicolored (red, green, yellow, orange) globe with the word *love* written on it in multiple languages

Styling the Stage

93

The team has labored over this graphic together, giving the colors and "feel" a lot of tweaking and reworking until everyone felt it made just the right statement, painted just the right picture. Since we associate Mexico with bright colors, we've opted to bring out the reds, greens, yellows, and oranges—all gel colors we've inserted into the lighting cans that will throw warm, ambient light up onto the back walls of the stage area. This careful attention to the lighting to pull out the main screen graphic colors literally transforms the environment of the large room. Its bright, warming presence invites worshippers to come in and take part. "Something good is going to

happen in here," the atmosphere whispers, and our prayer is that our people will experience a very rich worship encounter.

For stage décor, Lupina will bring maracas and some personal homeland collections for us to draw from. Another Ginghamsburg family has been to Mexico on mission numerous times, and we've asked them to bring any blankets, clothing, or other themed items they might have to offer. It's unusual for me not to know exactly what we'll end up with until Saturday, so I am feeling a bit anxious. But I'm trusting that we'll be able to pull it together with God's help. With the key colors in mind, we've already set aside red, orange, and yellow candles from our candle stash to use on candle stands of varying heights.

As I've mentally designed the stage, I know this celebration will have at least two great elements. I anticipate that the music, all planned with a Latin feel, will be nothing short of exciting. Early in the planning stages I asked Fran to schedule in an extra horn or two, and the songs will be fun and worshipful. (Yes, fun and worshipful can coexist!) I'm also excited about the video Todd will have produced, a retelling of our recent adult mission trip to Mexico. Because we connect throughout the week, I know the finished video will include the colors, music bed, and "feel" of our other worship elements. This combination of our best teamwork is *my* best translation of Romans 8:28: "And we know that in all things [design elements, media, artistic creations, musical selections] God works for the good of those who *love him*, who have been called according to *his purpose.*"

THE RESULTING EXPERIENCE

In the end, our Hispanic weekend was all we had hoped it would be. We were even allowed to bring chips and salsa into the worship area! The Latin-style music came alive. Todd's video featured our bright color scheme and a music bed with a Mexican feel. His digital story captured the adult mission team excitedly describing the home they had built from the ground up for a mother of six.

The stage displays included woven blankets, baskets, the colored candles, and various artifacts from Lupina, including her Spanish Bible. We placed a large piece of framed artwork (supplied by Lupina) on an easel flanked by candle stands at the main entrance to the worship area. Extending the worship-themed décor to the entryways, the lobby, and even the outside walkways when possible helps build anticipation for an exciting and meaningful worship experience.

Lupina's message was powerful as, with a thick Hispanic accent, she boldly described God's inclusive heart of love. Looking back, we did not simply hear a message from a Hispanic pastor. To be in the worship celebration that day was to *feel* the heartbeat of the Mexican people as we allowed ourselves to consider our own part in learning God's "language of love." All in all, It was a powerful cross-cultural, multisensory God experience.

Multisensory worship is a given at Ginghamsburg. It never fails to move us. But will it move you? Do you dare to try it in your own church?

Right now I'm pretty sure I hear someone saying, "Isn't God enough? Why do we need all this 'stuff' to create environment?" (Trust me...some weeks I'm tempted to ask that myself!) The truth is that while God may be temporarily "invisible" to us, God's creation is all around us—and it reflects the glory of God. God has gifted us with an unending palette of color and an incredible montage of humanity. In these things we catch glimpses of God's character. We only have to turn and look around our world to be reminded that our God is a God of amazing variety. Why not celebrate that variety in worship?

All of creation sings the glory of God. Each weekend we simply attempt to portray one small part of God's character. As human beings made in God's image, we use God's palette of color to brighten dark lives. We imitate God's

> As human beings made in God's image, we use God's palette of color to brighten dark lives. We imitate God's creative initiative toward humankind as we present the gospel using metaphor, parables, and real-life stories.

creative initiative toward humankind as we present the gospel using metaphors, parables, and real-life stories. In this we follow the example of Jesus, who often spoke in metaphors and frequently used visual imagery to describe timeless truth. "I will make you *fishers* of men," Jesus said (Matthew 4:19). "You are *the salt* of the earth" (Matthew 5:13). Styling the stage is simply our attempt to bring God's imagery to life, to provide for ourselves a place inside the story, to be in the moment with God.

CREATING SPACES

As you begin to re-create your own worship space, identify several places where key "anchor displays" could be arranged. It is impossible and unnecessary to redecorate an entire worship area. Most of the time I've found it best to focus on two or three key locations where visual displays would enhance the message. Not sure where to start? Try starting on the stage, perhaps in an area originally created for an altar-type arrangement. These displays are like modern-day altars, places where we can meet God and be reminded of God's presence and power.

In our environment we often create two anchor displays, one on either end of the large stage, and sometimes a smaller version closer to the center. This allows more people in the room to see and experience the display. Overall balance is important, so we look at the different "pieces" we'll have on the stage each weekend and allow what is happening with people to dictate décor placement. The band is usually fairly stationary, but we may have other people or props that require space in the stage area. Additional musicians, interview sets, a drama or a dance, a table with communion elements, or even stacks of the third-grade Bibles we give out once a year all require dedicated space. Each weekend's unique segments require us to constantly rethink our placement, always creating a fresh picture of worship. I love this challenge—"all-new day, all-new chances!" It's like getting a new worship space every single weekend, fifty-two times a year.

Sometimes our rearrangements become semipermanent. (Nothing is ever truly permanent here, except the truth of the message!) One weekend we decided we needed to change our balcony space. The balcony was a flat area where rows of minimally engaged participants had been expected to watch a TV monitor for their worship experience. We wanted to provide a more community-friendly environment, a cafe-type atmosphere. To create the change, we purchased every black metal patio table we could find in the entire Dayton area. We spread the tables throughout the balcony, lit a votive candle in the center of each one, and set our nicest chairs around them. We added a couple of strategically placed monitors and made drinks available for a minimal donation. The re-created worship seating is now much more hospitable than the rows of chairs had been.

Encouraged by our success in the balcony, we kept going! For our Saturday evening celebrations, we took out the last few rows of chairs in the main worship area and added twelve large, round tables across the back. We placed chairs around the tables so they would all face the front of the room. Seating space does not permit us to do this on Sunday mornings, but our Saturday evening crowd loves the new table seating! Worshippers grab the tables right away and enjoy the opportunity to gather and worship with a small group of friends.

About the time we were completing these semipermanent rearrangements, fellow worship designer Debbie Kasper visited Ginghamsburg. In addition to giving us feedback about Mike's teaching (see Chapter 3), Debbie also offered to share her insights about our worship environment. I was eager to hear how it appeared to her "fresh eyes." I wanted to know what she had *experienced*. Here's what Debbie had to say:

"The atmosphere with the tables and candles really created a more relaxed atmosphere. I don't know of many churches that have dared to bring tables and chairs into their main worship space."

Great things can happen when you dare to change. As you work to create new environments, however, always keep in mind the needs of your team members. In our experience, we've noticed that onstage team members such as speakers, drama players, or musicians can get a little anxious about "their space." They usually have a good idea of what kind of space (and how much space) they need to accomplish their roles in the service. If physical environment changes are in the works, it's best to talk over any special challenges ahead of time to avoid last-minute trauma. We try to promote an atmosphere of flexibility and encourage ourselves not to become too territorial. Being able to strategize together ahead of time seems to be the key. But even that hasn't totally eliminated what I refer to as...

DRAMA TRAUMA

Most worship areas have their unique challenges, and ours is no exception. We have no real dedicated drama space, so we've tried to think of the entire room as the actors' potential arena. We've used aisles, balcony space, center stage, and stage left, what we refer to as our "drama wing." (It sounds a lot more glamorous than it is.) Unfortunately, any drama set or furniture we might want to leave there permanently would prevent members of our deaf community from seeing the screen and prevent the audience from seeing the vocal ensemble. We keep working on new drama placement ideas, but for now this situation serves as a good reminder that we *all* have challenges to overcome and less than ideal circumstances to think through.

One Christmas Eve we staged two "modern-day angels" delivering monologues from two upper-ledge storage areas looking out over the audience—complete with fog-machine enhancement! (It was fairly effective, but I'm thinking now that it could have been illegal!) Once a very disturbed man came into a worship gathering and climbed onto the stage to verbally attack the speaker. Several worshippers later told us that they thought it was part of the drama! Since we have so many unique dramatic sets and scenarios, we've since promised to let our security team know when someone from the floor is *supposed* to come up onto the stage.

BEAUTY AND THE BUDGET: SUPPLIES FOR YOUR CREATIVE CLOSET

In order to produce dramas and style stages, you'll need props. Where are you going to get all these things? More importantly, once you find out where to get them, how are you going to pay for them? Although the physical enhancements I've described may seem costly, we've actually spent very little to obtain them. We're constantly asking ourselves, "What is already here that we can use for this purpose? What do we have that can find new life in a stage display?"

We use a few standard pieces (mostly homemade) over and over again to support the stage look each week. These pieces provide a framework or backdrop for any specific thematic pieces we might want to add. Here's a list of some basic pieces from our "closet of possibilities." The list describes the pieces we've found most helpful and how we made or acquired them.

STAGE PROPS

Black boxes. Years ago I realized that we were going to need some way to create displays on the stage. I started paying attention to the displays I'd seen in department stores and came upon the idea of the black box. Multiple boxes, each painted glossy black on five sides, with one end open. A Ginghamsburg servant-carpenter made ours out of half-inch plywood.

We now have six large black boxes (24x18x18-inch) and two smaller ones (18x12x12-inch). We can turn them, stack them, use them alone, or butt them up next to each other. We've used these black boxes for everything from stools for reader's theater to individual stands for communion elements. They also make handy table stands for extra musical equipment. They always look great on stage without distracting from the "professional" look. It's possible to purchase black boxes (made of plastic) from a catalog, but we made our own very economically and in just the sizes we needed. We repaint them every so often to keep them looking nice.

Old wooden crates serve as another alternative when we have box-type needs. We've acquired a large collection of these from a landscape nursery for next to nothing. These aged crates create a more natural, rough kind of look. While we can use them the same way as the black boxes, their distinct look communicates an entirely different message. Choices are good!

Antique communion table. While we used to use a large, fancy communion table, it always felt like "church hardware" to me. It was extremely formal looking (we're not very formal) and took up an enormous amount of the valuable floor space we needed for people. We've now relegated that larger table to wedding use only. In its place we purchased a smaller, simpler table from an antique store. The table top is wood, matching the crates. We painted the legs black to match the stage skirting and the black boxes. Since we have the freedom to move things around, we find endless ways to use this piece of stage furniture.

Old rugged cross. We don't have a cross hanging on the wall in our worship area, but we do have the option to use a cross as often as we want to. Our "old rugged cross" is 6x10-foot and probably made from old 4x4s. Because Scripture never specifies that the cross of Jesus was both upright and empty at the same time, I tried not to worry too much when the stand for this wooden cross suddenly disappeared one week. I began laying the cross on its side at an angle on the stage, propping it against black boxes or crates with cement blocks inside for stability.

We've placed the cross in a number of different places on the stage. Depending on what we were trying to communicate, we've arranged candles, draped cloth, or other supporting visual pieces around it. On communion weekends (the first weekend of each month), we frequently place broken bread and a goblet in front of the cross on a smaller box. These different arrangements cause us to consider the meaning of the cross in new ways, inviting greater appreciation for all that Jesus has done for us.

Urban cross. A few years ago we had a weekend when we needed a different kind of cross. We wanted a cross with less natural wood that would provide more of an "urban" feel to connect with our brothers and sisters in the city. We purchased metal signpost material and created a 5x7-foot cross. After painting it black, a Ginghamsburg servant created a stand by welding this cross to a large, circular metal base. Now we have the choice of two totally different crosses to enhance two kinds of looks, depending on the overall feel of the weekend.

LIGHTING

CANDLES. There are several things to keep in mind when using candles, the first being safety. Always check ahead of time for any potentially dangerous situations when you use candles. As much as possible, set candles away from the general flow of people traffic. If people are concerned about open flames, place clear glass hurricane covers over lit candles. We've always been able to work within these guidelines, and in nine years of creating multisensory worship settings, we have never had a fire. (We've had some humorous situations, but that's another book!) So far we've managed to provide safe spaces for ministry without losing that creative edge.

Candles are truly an effective piece of the overall multisensory experience. However, it can be costly to use candles week after week. We've developed a few ways to keep the cost down and the effectiveness up:

- **Watch for great sales.** As with everything you buy, make this your motto: *Never* pay full price!
- **Three-inch-wide candles** (sometimes called "chunky") **are best**. When cared for well, they burn for a long, long time. In contrast, tapers are fast burners in a room where air vent fans are blowing (our challenge), and fast-burning candles make a mess.
- **Color is important.** Flames burning inside large, dark-colored candles cannot be seen from a distance (lessening their effectiveness for use on stage). Lighter colors such as whites and yellows cause the flame inside the candle to appear as a dancing glow, which maximizes its effectiveness.
- **Very hard, more expensive candles** will last longer and may be the best way to go if purchased on sale.
- **Trimming longer wicks** to about one-half inch each time the candles are lit will keep the candles from producing smoky flames. Some candles

may also need the wax to be poured out from time to time.

- *Placing a sheet of fabric, paper, plastic, or plexiglass* under the candle stands will prevent wax from spilling onto the carpet below. If wax does drip onto fabric or carpet, you can repair the damage by (1) scraping the excess wax off the surface, (2) placing paper towels over the spot and ironing with a hot iron (the paper towels will blot up the wax), and (3) writing a note of apology to the custodian or housekeeping personnel.

CANDLE STANDS. Candle stands have become an absolute must for creating any sort of intimate worship gathering. Usually found in sets of varying heights, they can be used over and over again. We may change the candles and placement from week to week, but scarcely a weekend goes by that we do not use our candle stands in some way. On communion weekends, we use them to highlight the cross. Some weeks we space them evenly across the front of the stage; other weeks they create a backdrop for a vocal ensemble. Candle stands elevate lit candles so they can be seen from quite a distance. Even worshippers just entering the room can see the lit candles and immediately feel welcomed.

Inquiring minds usually want to know where to find candle stands at modest prices. Depending on your geographic location, I would suggest Pier 1 Imports (wait for a sale!), Value City, Sam's Club, and Kirklands (Costco). Various Web sites and boutiques can be helpful as well. (My motto: Always be on the lookout for cool, cheap stage stuff!) Buying several sets of candle stands allows for flexible and portable display options, and the initial investment will provide long-term benefit. Candle stands can also be used by others in the church for weddings and funerals, and should be stored in or near…

- *A dedicated candle closet.* Storing sets of colored candles together in a closet or large cupboard is very helpful and will encourage others in your church to use candles for their events. Labeled shelves enable different ministry groups to use the candles, then return them to their proper places (so you can find them when you need them!). We always hope others will take advantage of our candle closet, because at Ginghamsburg we don't encourage multisensory worship only; we also encourage multisensory ministry!

PIN LIGHTS are actually small "can" lights that are available through commercial lighting catalogs. Some more industrial-looking displays are most effectively enhanced with spotlighting rather than candles. We keep six pin spots on hand that we can plug in on location to throw a small ray of focused light onto key areas. Colored "gel" paper can be inserted into the pin lights to change their effect.

LANTERNS are a great décor possibility and are often available through craft stores, Odd Lots, or Pottery Barn. Hanging lanterns at varying heights creates a great ambience, but for a while we didn't know how to accomplish this—which brings me to the last item in our creative closet…

LARGE "SHEPHERD HOOK" LANTERN STANDS. We needed to hang nine lanterns one Christmas (we'd found them at Odd Lots). We also needed a very cost-effective way to hang them. A talented Ginghamsburg servant created hanger stands for us out of rebar, the textured metal rod used in reinforced concrete. (This can be purchased at a lumber store.)

The rebar was shaped into a shepherd's hook at the top, with a small "v" turned up on the very end to accommodate a lantern handle. To make the hooks free-standing, he added a three-pronged base at the bottom, formed by welding three 12-inch pieces of rebar together. We now have three sets of differing heights. Although originally intended for the lantern service, we later discovered other uses for these stands. We now use them to hang signs, drape fabric, or suspend strings of lights. Maybe additional uses are coming to your mind as you're reading!

Sometimes these standard pieces from our closet are all it takes to create the environment for our worship celebrations. Sometimes we add a few others. By mixing and matching these simple items in different ways, we're able to create a vast array of worship environments. Creating beauty on a budget is entirely possible!

ACQUIRING THE UNUSUAL WITHOUT OPENING THE WALLET

As we dream big worship dreams, we sit around the table and visualize the resulting worship service. And then we have to stop and ask ourselves, "Wait a minute—how on earth are we going to make *that* happen?" How are we going to persuade the amusement park to allow our videographer and his equipment inside? How are we going to get those motorcycles parked on the stage? How is this forty-something mother of three going to get up the courage to show up at a sky diving appointment and jump out of an airplane? With God's help—that's how.

Over time we've really come to trust that with God's help, it *will* happen, oh yes, it will. To allow ourselves the escape route of "maybe it's just not God's will" simply provides an easy way out. We don't dare think that might be true until five o'clock on Saturday when the first weekend celebration begins. Up until then, we keep trying. Many weeks we've had to really rack our brains to figure it all out, but when God helps us succeed, the rewards are great.

A few weeks back, we wanted to tell the story of the woman at the well. We had a great script adapted from John 4. We had a storyteller but, alas, no well. "Where to find a well?" we wondered. Finding one seemed an expensive and impossible goal, since none of us had a clue about where to look. "Let's make our own," our summer worship intern suggested. And we went for it!

We gathered about thirty cement blocks and formed them into a four-foot-wide circle, three layers high. We found rounded, red decorative bricks in the Ginghamsburg garage to place in the wedge-shaped cracks between the blocks. We got a really thick rope out of my garage, threw one end into the "well," and wrapped the other end around the handle of an old wooden bucket. *Voilà*, a well! A place for our storyteller to inhabit while telling about Jesus' encounter with the Samaritan woman.

Water always seems to inspire us to do great things. One weekend Mike chose to talk about our Living Water, available as a contin-uous source of refreshment (John 4:10-14). We called the service "Thirsty." We thought about using water in the environment. We *dreamed* about using running water. I had seen a shop in Tipp City that had small, decorative water fountains with running water. I knew we could never afford those fountains at over a hundred dollars each. So I asked the store's owner if we could borrow them for our worship display. She said that we could, and she and I brainstormed together how our stage team might pick them up and return them to the shop without her losing valuable sales time. (I like creating win-win partnerships.)

Every corner of the worship area that weekend was multisensory. We set up fountains in the entryway and on the stage. Between celebrations, we played a CD with sounds of flowing water and a moving-water animation graphic on the screen. (Did a lot of people leave worship to use the restroom, or did I just imagine that?) We acquired the unusual without opening the wallet.

A few months ago, Mike wanted to preach about our need for the full armor of God but wanted to update it somehow. This presented just the kind of challenge that our team loves. "How about an 'Armor of God' fashion show?" I suggested. "We could feature each piece on individual models." The team agreed on the direction, and we called it "Dressed for Success." We used these elements:

- 🌐 **Word:** Ephesians 6:10-17
- 🌐 **Felt Need:** I'm too vulnerable in my humanity to be successful.
- 🌐 **Desired Outcome:** Participants will get dressed (with the full armor of God)
- 🌐 **Theme:** Dressed for Success
- 🌐 **Look:** Runway and a glitzy fashion show with models wearing armor pieces.

Wednesday afternoon we began searching for armor by calling Christian supply stores. Finally, at a party costume shop, we found a plastic breastplate, shield, belt, and helmet. All of these armor accessories were metallic gold and silver. So we spray painted an old pair of boots gold and borrowed a samurai sword—armor complete. (These pieces weren't all free, granted, but the cost was fairly minimal.)

Mike had been careful in Wednesday's team meeting to explain the usefulness of each piece of armor. We developed a character for each armor item. I wrote a "Call to Wardrobe" drama script. On Friday, a team reconfigured the stage to create a runway out into the congregation. (Our staging pieces are like LEGO building blocks—you can build whatever you imagine!) The band introduced the drama with the ZZ Top song "Sharp Dressed Man." Todd made a little behind-the-scenes video to set it up, featuring the models arguing in the makeshift dressing room. Cheryl Wyatt narrated in her best French accent. Everyone really got into it, and once we'd edged the stage and runway with little white minilights (your Christmas closet!) it definitely did not look like a typical worship area. Truthfully, I had a tiny fear that we had really gone over the top this time.

In the end, much to our surprise, *everyone* loved it. Old people loved it; young people loved it. (Try it sometime in your congregation—you'll find the script in the Appendix.) I believe the reason we didn't receive even one com-

plaint about going "over the top" was that the spiritual message, our desperate human need for God armor in the battle of life, was so powerful that it felt like God's hand was all over that celebration. It's the only way to explain it. It felt great that all of us (the drama players, the singers, the band, the lighting and camera teams) were able to use our gifts in such an out-of-the-box kind of way. The congregation was edified, realizing the kind of God clothing we all have available, and God was truly honored in our discovery.

OK, so we *are* a little crazy and we *do* go to extremes once in a while. But after all is said and done, worship is something we can and should give our lives to. This is the most awesome community to work among, because we have the greatest story to tell. It's invigorating to know that we've created something together that will influence lives for years to come. We've dreamed the unusual to accomplish the impossible. "I can do everything through him who gives me strength" (Philippians 4:13).

ASK, SEEK, KNOCK

We could have said no when we couldn't figure out where to get a well, how to find the armor, or where to go for running water. When no is not an option, we'll all work a lot harder to make things happen—and we'll be helped by the One who's promised to do *exceedingly and abundantly* more than all we ask or think!

> "Now to him who is able to do im-
> measurably more than all we ask or
> imagine, according to his power that
> is at work within us, to him be
> glory in the church and in Christ
> Jesus throughout all generations, for
> ever and ever!" (Ephesians 3:20-21)

When you encounter challenges in worship planning, discouragement can easily set in. We all get discouraged, but we don't have to stay discouraged. Staying discouraged wastes valuable time. Keep asking, keep seeking, and keep working toward the goal: powerful God experiences!

CHAPTER 11

Focusing on the Inside Story

"Make visible what, without you, might perhaps never have been seen."

ROBERT BRESSON

Dreaming and teaming effective media pieces for worship celebrations have been a very natural part of our weekly process. Most of our team players are not media experts by any stretch of the imagination. We're just life livers. We dabble in media because they afford us the opportunity to bring more human life, more people stories, more of God's creation, more culture and candor into our worship experience.

Media are powerful tools that invite us into life scenarios we may not have previously experienced for ourselves. Without media, it's easy for people to begin to think, "Life is all about me." Yet when I *see* a homeless person on the screen as I hear U2's "Beautiful Day," I am reminded that "there but for the grace of God go I." When I *see* the story of a mom who lost her teenage daughter to a train collision, I am reminded to be thankful for my daughter, who is alive. I am reminded to pray for this mom, Dee Todd, whose daughter is with Jesus, and I realize that life is not always fair but that God's love is unchanging. (Dee Todd's story can be viewed on the video resource *Art & Soul,* volume 2, and is available from the Ginghamsburg e-store at www.ginghamsburg.org.) Media allow us into the lives and experiences of other people.

When we shared the video of my own sky diving experience in our worship celebrations, I took three thousand people up ten thousand feet into the air with me, and then we all jumped out of a plane—together. ("Jump" is available on the *Visual Edge* visual resource through Group Publishing, Inc.,

P.O. Box 481, Loveland, CO 80539.)
We experienced the Green County,
Ohio, landscape; the rush of the chute
opening up; the relief of the soft land-
ing—together. Media in their best forms
bring the outside world into our worship
area. We experience it, connect it to
God's message, and then take that message back out.

Todd Carter, our videographer, understands this need for connection.
Todd is a media soldier. He's in early every morning; he stays late if need be.
He always finds the story, and he doesn't let up until his own perspiration
evokes our congregational inspiration. Spend a few moments with me as we
get the "inside story" from Todd.

SERVANT INTERVIEW

Todd Carter

KIM: *After working in secular media, you
chose to pursue media as a ministry. How
is media ministry different from secular
media, and what do you find the most
fulfilling about it?*

TODD: In media ministry we're called to make local heroes out of the people in
our congregation—to use media to communicate God's truth in a message
that isn't smiley, happy sunshine all the time. We certainly want to give a perspective on the world, but the important thing is communicating God's
truth. Rather than feeling like I'm communicating the "crime and slime" that
people like to watch (with all its sensationalism), I'm communicating that in
the *midst* of the crime and slime, we have this flower that's growing, and it's
called hope for people's lives. We are able to find those bright points and
communicate, "You know what? The world around us does have tons of
problems, but God is alive and doing new things. And we are here to celebrate that!" Media are great tools for that kind of communication in the age
that we live in now. That's our mission, I think: to help communicate—not
really to offset what we see in the world, but to communicate on a whole
other level.

KIM: *You're known for capturing a great story and making heroes out of everyday followers of Jesus. What components do you most want to include in a great digital storytelling?*

TODD: Stories can be told in many different ways. I think most stories have a "hook" of some kind, some aspect that makes you say, "OK, I can see myself in that." It's down on a level where it's something that could happen to you. It's communicating basic things that happen to everybody in a way that makes people feel, "Hey, that could be me. This is what I can do or become." That kind of story is relevant.

There are many types of stories, but you always want a climax. You can take a piece that seems to be going one way but ends up going a completely different direction, sort of a "bait-and-switch," or you can have a story that is never resolved. We try to do stories that focus on real-life, everyday people that are just doing the best that they can in their Jesus journey. We communicate where they were before, where they are today, what happened (the "hook"), and where they see themselves going. It's kind of the old testimony-type format.

Many stories can be told really well. It's like writing a paper where you take lots of different bits and pieces of information and somehow put them together in a cohesive way. It's almost like a puzzle where the pieces all fit together to make a whole. When that happens, it's magic.

KIM: *I've seen these video stories over and over. I know where the "hook" is for me because that's where I get teary-eyed. I'll see a daughter in a graduation gown kissing her mom, hearing that something difficult has happened in their lives, and it speaks to me. So it becomes* my *story too, because I feel the connection. That's how God works through media.*

TODD: There is no cookie-cutter format that makes a story work. You have to let the story tell itself and unveil it as it happens. If a story touches not only your head but also your heart, then chances are that you are just getting out of the way and letting God do the work as the story tells itself. That's the best way to tell a story. Approach it not as "this is what the story has to have," but "this is what the story is."

KIM: *That says a lot about postmodern ministry and how to tell the stories along the path. You just zoom in on one person that's on the path and get the story, and then zoom in another day on another person. Pretty soon, you notice that transformation is happening along the path in real people's lives. How do you know when a video piece has gone beyond information to transformation?*

TODD: I don't know if I can really explain it, but I know I can feel it. If you've ever watched a movie or television show and had tears well up or felt an intense emotion, you know the show was an effective form of communication. In school we did an experiment. We watched a film in a different language and could only hear the music, sense the dialogue, and view the action. The story was communicated just by the acting. Tears came to our eyes. We didn't understand what they were saying, but we knew that in some sense, we felt it. Whenever you can go beyond your head to your heart, it becomes an effective communication piece. It's transforming.

KIM: *So effective media should evoke emotion in some way.*

TODD: Yes…inspiration or passion that says, "I can do that," or "That's amazing, I never knew that. Now I'm going to go tell the people I saw in that video that they were inspiring to me, that they're pushing me out of my comfort zone because I know *they're* doing it." Those kinds of things are not necessarily pieces you can put handles to, but when you feel it, you know it's transforming your life.

KIM: *What's the best feedback you've received after a person has viewed one of your stories?*

TODD: I remember doing the Break Forth Canada conference in Edmonton, Alberta, Canada. We showed a video of a family from Ginghamsburg whose daughter was born with Trisomy 18, a genetic chromosomal defect causing the child to have a shortened life expectancy. A mother in the workshop actually left the room after viewing the video. She came back fifteen minutes later. Afterward she came up to me and said, "You know what? My own daughter was born with Trisomy 18, and up until this point, I felt like no one totally understood me. I had no idea that anyone with a faith background had ever dealt with anything like this. I cannot tell you how much it means to me to be able to see hope in a family who is approaching this as I am. I can't tell you how comforting that is."

I connected her with that family in our church and they began e-mailing back and forth. I think they even went to a convention somewhere together and met face to face. They exchange information and pictures and have developed a friendship even though they are thousands of miles away from each other. The relationship is based on their stories and what God is doing through the miracle of their children. So to me, it really wasn't so much about the medium as it was about the message. When the medium is as invisible as it can be but the message is powerful, you know it's effective and will transform people. That video piece is a great example of inspiration and transformation. For me, it's not about the medium. It's about the church being transformed.

KIM: *Videos are powerful because they can have as much impact the tenth time they are viewed as they did the first time for a different audience. That video story lived on and connected people that would never have known each other. That's awesome, Todd. In what ways do you think you see life differently than others?*

TODD: I'm always thinking in terms of what can be a good hook or connection. I am always thinking of ideas for transforming one medium into another. I may see an effective print ad and say, "I wonder if I could transform this into an electronic, visual kind of medium."

KIM: *What would you say to someone who really wants to do serious media ministry in his or her church? Are there some "always" and "never-dos" in media ministry?*

TODD: It's difficult to classify the "always" and "nevers." Media ministry is an art, and where there is art, there are rarely rules of *do* or *do not*. There are a few things that I would *suggest* to do or not to do. One is to try not to be afraid of your screen. That's usually the tendency when you first try to implement a media ministry. Some say, "We'll use it only for the sermon and then turn it off. Why use it for songs?" Others may decide to use it for songs but nothing else.

KIM: *There is nothing uglier than a blank screen.*

TODD: Exactly! There really is no such thing as the screen being "off." If it's off, it's just black or gray. That is communicating too. What it's saying is "The lights are on, but nobody's home!" It communicates that no one cares and that it is not important enough for someone to put a lot of time into this.

Be careful what you are communicating. If you don't have a lot of time or haven't found the people in your church to make that happen, choose one piece of great art that matches the overall idea and leave it on the screen. It will serve as your stained-glass window. It will implant in people's minds a picture of the one thing you truly wanted to communicate that week. Given that, the screen would still be a very effective use of communication. That is one thing you could consider an "always."

Another "always" is that a team-based ministry is important. You can't do ministry on your own over the long haul. If it depends solely upon one person, you may start out really well, but I don't believe you could sustain it long-term. It would also keep you from growing. Team is hugely important.

Always ask yourself, "What are the new technologies? What have I seen here? What have I seen there? How can I adapt this to fit into my style?" You're not necessarily trying to copy what other churches are doing, but rather thinking in terms of leaving the door open to new, creative ideas that have never been done.

Sometimes it works; sometimes it doesn't. If you're not willing to try, you're never going to go beyond where you are right now. Trust me; we've been there. We say, "Well, we learned what not to do this time." Sometimes things haven't worked out quite the way we planned, and we wouldn't do it that way again. But we wouldn't have known if we hadn't tried. You can't be afraid of failure.

KIM: *That's great insight, because people do become fearful when new technology is introduced.*

TODD: Technology is not the devil—although it does seem to be possessed at certain times. Even if you don't know it or have time to learn it, find someone in the church who does; then turn that person loose to see what he or she can come up with.

KIM: *Anything else you would add?*

TODD: There are so many different ways to communicate visually in our churches. A lot of churches have screens, projectors, and media capability. Technology is progressing, and we're only seeing the beginning of what could prove to be a creative revolution in the church.

I believe we are going to see major growth and endless possibilities. What used to cost thousands of dollars five years ago is now more affordable. With home computers, everybody can be an editor. Family reunions, vacations, and first birthdays are captured on DVD. It's amazing to see the progression of media and where they're headed. It's a great time to be in the church!

KIM: *Thanks, Todd. I hope there's a movie in heaven about all the lives that have been changed through your work.*

We live in a media-saturated world. Everywhere we look, we're surrounded by media. We can't escape or hide from them. But we can harness their power for God's best purposes. Through digital storytelling, graphic imagery, worshipful art, mission moments (videos highlighting various ministries or projects), and myriad other forms, we can elevate this earthly form to an eternal function. And as we do so, God will be glorified.

CHAPTER 12

Playing to the Heart of Our Colorful God

"He taught me how to sing the latest God-song,

a praise-song to our God.

More and more people are seeing this:

they enter the mystery,

abandoning themselves

to God."

(PSALM 40:3, THE MESSAGE)

Two or three hours into every design team meeting, Fran Wyatt, our music director, will inevitably ask this question: "What is the *vibe* we're going for here this week?"

It's an excellent question. I *love* that question. It's proof positive that designing powerful God experiences goes way beyond the cerebral to something much deeper inside of us. It's a question that invites us to begin describing the worship celebration to one another in terms like *edgy, high-feel, ancient-future, cartoonlike, nostalgic, industrial,* or *earthy*, just to name a few. (We make these up as we go along!)

When the team agrees on the *vibe*, I know more about how to style the stage. Todd can decide better how to treat the videos. Brent understands how to design the graphics. And most of all, Fran knows which songs to choose. We've also learned that God is not limited to any particular vibe. God can work through them all.

Music is a powerful form of connection and communication. It plays to both sides of the brain at the same time. The tones keep the right side busy so the messages can be absorbed into the left. Our team works hard to identify the musical styles and themes that will enable the maximum number of people to connect...into the celebration, into the message, and, ultimately, into Jesus.

How is it possible to find and play music that will communicate the depth of God's love for us? I interviewed Fran to find out.

SERVANT INTERVIEW
Fran Wyatt

KIM: *Fran, you're thirty-eight. In your wildest life dreams, did you ever expect you'd be sitting here talking about being the music director of a large church? A large, mostly white church?*

FRAN: Not at all. As a matter of fact, it's probably the last thing that I could ever think of that I would be doing at this time.

KIM: *How do you think God has used you so far with this particular congregation? Where do you see that we've come as a result of the music since you've been here?*

FRAN: I hope that we've begun to understand the African-American culture a little bit better. Because this is a predominately white congregation, I'm sure there were a few preconceived ideas about what it means to be African-American. Hopefully, I have helped us to understand that there are probably not as many differences as we might think, and things that are different are things that can be embraced by all. It's important to musically stretch the palette a little bit. It helps people experience rap, gospel, blues, and R & B in a different light, to be able to appreciate it and realize that God is able to speak through other forms of music as well as what we're used to hearing.

KIM: *Do you think our worship is deepening here?*

FRAN: I think so. Maybe because we're changing and worshipping in a different way than what other churches might be or what people had previously seen as comfortable. It's definitely a different style of worship.

KIM: *From where I sit, it feels like we're all singing more.*

FRAN: Does it? Sometimes it's a little hard to tell from the platform. I definitely think it is a different *type* of worship; maybe that's what you're hearing.

KIM: *What is multicultural music? What does that really mean?*

FRAN: I think it means that throughout the course of a celebration, there would be some song that, no matter what cultural background you came from, you could latch on to and take home with you. A song that causes you to say, "Hey, that really spoke to me. I was able to connect to it." It means to provide different hooks that people can latch on to. It may not be exactly the way you heard the song before, but something about it is familiar—whether it's the words, the sound, or the melody. It means something to you no matter what culture you come from.

KIM: *We are doing a "flying" theme this weekend. Tell us how you managed to figure out some multicultural music for this celebration.*

FRAN: With the flying theme, the first thing that came to my mind was the song "Fly Like an Eagle," which was done by the Steve Miller Band. Because Steve Miller did it, it will connect with one group of people. But since Seal, an R & B group, covered it eight or nine years ago, it will connect with another group as well. The song has also been covered by a few jazz artists in the last couple of years. That will connect with another group. So with one song, three totally different people groups will be able to recognize the song and connect with it.

Throughout the celebration, my concept is to make sure that at least one of the songs will connect with everyone. "Hallelujah" will connect more to the CCM (contemporary Christian music) crowd, yet with the nature of our band, it will take on a more R & B flavor with acoustic guitar added. It's really a mesh of styles all together. Not necessarily doing a funk or country tune, but combining funk and country elements together. People really relate to it. And then there's "Sanctuary," which is a gospel-natured song. This creates a lot of places for people to connect.

KIM: *"Sanctuary" was probably a little hard for us when we first did it here, but I love doing that one now. It feels really interactive to me.*

FRAN: I would say the whole call and response thing is very different for a predominately white congregation, because the call and response is a tradition from the African-American church. I think when we first asked our people to do it, they were a little scared and uncomfortable. But the more we did it, the more they started to enjoy it.

KIM: *And then we're wrapping it up with "Amazing Grace," which anybody that's ever been to a church, and even some who haven't, would know. That's a connection too.*

FRAN: Yes. The fact that we're going to be doing it a cappella at the end also helps to connect with the more traditionalists. Even though we may start out more hip-hop and funky, it will end up being a cappella at the right point in time. Once again, it's finding ways to connect several groups of people with the same song as opposed to trying to do eight or nine songs to hit everybody. You don't have time to do that. You find ways to connect more people into what's going on with fewer songs.

KIM: *Why does the church need to pursue multicultural anything, including music?*
FRAN: Because it represents the true picture of the kingdom of heaven. There is so much that can be learned from different cultures. I am who I am because of a combination of everything I've learned—from Greek, Hispanic, African-American, and Caucasian cultures. Thinking back as a child from the age of nine years on, I was always in an integrated situation. My mom made sure of that, and I've learned so much more from that kind of upbringing. It can be very easy to get caught up in just what you understand. When we start to branch out into different cultures, we start to understand more. My encouragement is that we don't just stop when we understand ourselves, but that we seek to understand others as well.

KIM: *What do you love to find in a musician?*
FRAN: Passion! First and foremost is passion. It's not so much about being technically proficient; however, I do truly appreciate that. But I've heard many technically advanced musicians whose passion stops for no apparent reason when they pick up the instrument. I've heard musicians who've had limited proficiency of the instrument, and yet are somehow able to communicate exactly how they feel at that moment with passion. So for me, the first thing I look for in musicians is passion. Once they have passion, you can teach them everything else. You can teach them how to play better, faster, and with more advanced harmonies, but it is very hard to teach passion.

KIM: *What challenges you about typical church music?*
FRAN: I see the whole idea of replicating something else to the T as a challenge. Many churches get a praise CD or hear someone doing a worship song and try to duplicate it exactly as they heard it. What they don't take into account is that what they heard was a combination of the different people who were performing it. It is a unique chemistry that *those* people created. Churches need to realize that when they do the song, they need to find the chemistry that will be created by *their* musicians and vocalists

along with the speaker. The speaker is going to be a big part of what comes out; the speaker's character and vision are going to be part of the whole scene. It's important to look at that recording only as a place to start and then ask, "God, where is our chemistry in this song? How do we make this come alive for us and *our* congregation?"

KIM: *What is your next dream for your life?*

FRAN: My desire right now is not just to become a better worship leader or a better musician, but to try to find a way to lift up all those around me. I'm realizing that "rising tides raise all ships." It's been on my mind a lot lately. My desire right now is not necessarily to hook up with a great artist. What I would love is to somehow take those around me who have felt they'd never be known for playing music and somehow, with God's help, elevate them to where they are living out a dream come true—a dream that goes far beyond their perceived limitations. I enjoy helping B players become A players and helping C players become B players. I know that is what I am called to do—to lift everybody around me up and *create* something great, as opposed to trying to go out and *find* something great.

KIM: *Thanks, Fran. You're just the right person for the job.*

I love the music at Ginghamsburg. I love the way it's stretching us and growing us into a multicultural community. I love how music can take my sagging spirit and pump the power of God right in. I am drawn into worship the moment the music begins.

Recently, a new follower of Jesus at Ginghamsburg told us his story. He told our staff that he is Jewish, an introverted man who never pictured himself in a Christian faith community. His cell group is his new family (his extended family is not pleased over his newfound faith), and he loves worshipping with the larger Ginghamsburg body. This man told us that every weekend he wants to run up and hug Fran right after worship because God moved so powerfully in his heart through the music he experienced. Music is a powerful part of worship. Our prayer is that our playing would touch the heart of our colorful God.

PART FIVE:

Messages That Move Hearts and Transform Lives

The spoken word is a powerful tool. Recently, our leadership board interviewed a man in anticipation of his joining the board. When asked to tell us how long he'd been at Ginghamsburg Church and why he was there, he related this story…

I began coming three years ago. I'd been in a church all my life, but that particular church was not a warm, accepting community. I had been recently divorced, which elicited a harsh response from those whose support I needed the most.

During my first worship experience at Ginghamsburg, I heard our pastor say that prechurched or unchurched people matter to God. Not nonchurched, but prechurched people. This gave me unbelievable hope. It said to me that no one was exempt from entry into God's kingdom. It communicated that there is hope and possibility for every single person to enter into faith. I knew at that moment that this was the church for me— a place where I could start my new life in Christ.

Words *are* powerful, and we must never underestimate what God can do when the spoken word intersects with the power of the Holy Spirit. Designing worship has helped me to discover that every passage of Scripture has a message. Every message has a story, a metaphor, or a look. Every story has a setting. Each weekend's message has a different slant, a different way of describing, explaining, or demonstrating the gospel. In this section we'll examine the ways that the messages we communicate can truly move hearts and transform lives.

CHAPTER 13

Writing for Worship Connection

"I am a little pencil in the hand of a writing God who is sending a love letter to the world."

MOTHER TERESA

It's 11:31 at night and time for David Letterman. I'm a news junkie, and I've just finished watching the 11:00 news when I see the camera pan over the Hudson River and across the New York City skyline. "Late Show with David Letterman" appears in that familiar font, and I hear the announcer introduce the show in that familiar voice. Not three seconds pass before I hear the "hook"—the names of the guests to be on the show that night. It is in those first ten seconds that I decide, "Should I stay or should I go? Should I watch Dave, switch over to Leno, or just give it up and go to sleep?" This is all within the first ten seconds of the show.

It's 10:33 on Sunday morning. Monty Postmodern is sitting close to the center aisle, halfway back in the worship area. The opening music has just concluded and a "worship host" walks to the center stage, picks up the microphone, and begins to speak—and it's in those first ten seconds that Monty will decide whether he should stay or go.

At least that's how I try to think about it. That's the kind of importance I assign to the work of writing the connection pieces for worship celebrations. And while Monty and any of his postmodern pew-partners may not physically get up and leave the worship area, in the remote control of his mind he has full ability to press the channel button up or down and think about breakfast, lunch, golf, or tomorrow's presentation at the office.

The mind, however, is a terrible thing to waste. And if Monty has gone to the trouble of getting dressed for church, piling his children into the car, and finding a parking space, I want to make sure that we've done all we can to make his efforts worthwhile. My mission is to connect people to Jesus in creative ways, and I figure we're not going to get a second chance to make a powerful first impression.

REACH OUT AND TOUCH

Writing connection pieces for worship celebrations presents a significant opportunity to verbally "reach out and touch." Whether we're writing a call to worship, a prayer of confession, an interview, a drama, communion words, or announcements, what we say and how we say it will make all the difference in the world as we design powerful worship experiences. If God is "not wanting anyone to perish, but everyone to come to repentance" (2 Peter 3:9b), then we must passionately partner with God to "take captive every thought to make it obedient to Christ."

> "The weapons we fight with are not weapons of the world. On the contrary, they have divine power to demolish strongholds. We demolish arguments and every pretension that sets itself up against the knowledge of God, and we take captive every thought to make it obedient to Christ" (2 Corinthians 10:4-5).

As writers and communicators, it is our task to focus people's minds and hearts on what God truly wants to say to them. That is why even these connecting pieces must always be message-centered and thoughtfully prepared.

> "If then I do not grasp the meaning of what someone is saying, I am a foreigner to the speaker, and he is a foreigner to me" (1 Corinthians 14:11).

When I write a call to worship, I think about the big picture of the worship celebration and where we want to go, then ask how we might best grab our people's attention. Here are the elements I try to include:
- the felt need (a hook, question, statement)
- the desired outcome of the celebration
- the word or a small portion of it

- the theme with a graphic
- a segue into the song celebration or other next segment

For example, we recently introduced our new student ministry team and its plans to our congregation. Mike wanted to talk about our responsibility as parents, pastors, and providers to make sure our kids have every opportunity to journey with Jesus. The theme we chose was "Road Rules." We opened the celebration with "Teach Your Children" (Crosby, Stills, Nash, and Young), and then the host said these words as our call to worship:

"If life is a journey, then there's got to be some rules of the road. Rules that keep us on track with the One who called himself the way, the truth, and the life. The greatest trust that you and I have is to pass these road rules on to our children.

"Listen to how God calls us in Deuteronomy, chapter 11 (slightly paraphrased): 'Teach your children well. Fix my words on your hearts and minds, and then talk about them when you sit at home and when you walk along the road together, when you lie down and when you get up. Write them wherever they will be seen, so that you and your children may be blessed,' because ultimately, we all want to live life just like Jesus."

The carefully chosen words of this call to worship began by introducing the theme and ended by introducing our first worship song, an original song that Fran wrote called "Just Like You." In place of a traditional call to worship, you can also start off with a drama or a story that introduces the felt need, followed by a simple transition into a prayer or song.[1]

No matter what words we use, it's important to keep making sense and keep connecting the dots. Even announcements will take on new meaning when they are connected to the overall message. Anything that we use congregational time for should pertain to everyone in some way. Here's an example: "Next weekend's Community Festival is our biggest outreach opportunity of the year as we seek to 'bring seeking people to a life-Celebration of Jesus,' which is the first part of our mission statement here at Ginghamsburg. We want to be getting the word out to friends, neighbors, and co-workers about this exciting event!" Information that applies only to certain groups is better shared in writing or on a church Web site if you have one.

When a church is moving forward in mission together, the announcements are simply action steps toward the mission. We use announcements as part of our constant, strategic, and intentional communication about where we're going as a movement. When we connect these messages to the mission, we witness a surge in its momentum.

LESS IS MORE

If I've heard Mike say this once, I've heard him say it seven thousand times. We remind ourselves of this timeless principle in all the communication we do, whether we're creating media pieces, writing an all-church letter, planning a song celebration, or writing connecting pieces for worship.

Great communication is always using words wisely and never overestimating the attention span of the listener. When I write, I put myself in the pews and think about what it would take to engage me, to give me enough information and inspiration to keep me connected, but not so much that I become bored. *Less is more.*

A COMMON LANGUAGE

Learning to write for connection is a process, but the key for me was learning to speak what I call Ginghamese. Every church needs a language that evolves out of its DNA. For instance, we don't have volunteers at Ginghamsburg; we have unpaid servants. We don't hold worship services; we prepare for worship celebrations. We try to use regular language and avoid "churchy" words. We use active, persuasive verbs. We keep it positive; we never resort to guilt-inducing verbal techniques. We say "us" and "we" instead of "me" and "you." We affirm. We try to draw attention to God and God's unpaid servants rather than the speakers on the stage. With words, we tell people that they are accepted...they are *us*. Words tell people that with God, there is no male or female, Jew or Greek, black or white, young or old—that we all have a place at the table of God.

I encourage you to reflect on your own church's DNA and consider the language choices that might best support it. Language is important!

INTEGRATING THE PIECES

In order to ensure that multisensory worship connects with participants, we must take extra time to pull the pieces together. This is more artistically known as *integration*. Our team has a lot of ways we describe this connection: terrific transitions, smooth segues, setting one another up, handing it off.

Even though we might have exceptional individual pieces, if something is not in the right spot at the right time, if there is no context for why it is being presented, or if any segment is preceded or followed by a dead spot, its effectiveness can be lost. Multisensory worship is integrated worship; pieces overlap. Each piece builds on the last and prepares for the next.

Different teams will have different ways of engaging in the integration process. At Ginghamsburg, we draw up our initial worship plans on the whiteboard on Wednesday in room 202. Then I take the plans home and really think about them. I try to imagine myself in the room and think how it will look, feel, and connect. (It's not unusual for my husband to ask me on a Friday night, "How *was* worship this coming weekend?" He knows there's a sense that I've been there already!) Questions I ask myself and my team members as we work toward integration include these:

> If we lose our audience due to a distraction or a dead spot, it takes twenty minutes to fully get them back. We don't have twenty minutes to give away in any given worship celebration. Integrated, seamless worship eliminates distraction.

- How will that *feel*?
- How will it *feel* to have that rocky song blast out of nowhere?
- How will it *feel* to bow in a prayer of confession when I don't yet realize I've done anything wrong?
- How effective will it *feel* to have an altar call for salvation when the message was about reaching out to serve others?

Part of designing worship to be multisensory means unlearning "the way we've always done it." As we move toward integration, we've got to unlearn the way we've always considered various worship pieces as separate units. Separate pieces allow time for distraction. We want the pictures and stories to speak for themselves. If we lose our audience due to a distraction or a dead spot, it takes twenty minutes to fully get them back. We don't have twenty minutes to give away in any given worship celebration. Integrated, seamless worship eliminates distraction.

Maximizing each moment is essential. Here are some ways you can maximize the worship experience by integrating the pieces:

• Provide the host or worship leader with prepared lines that close one segment ("Amen," "Good to worship together") and segue into the next ("Coming up, some Lenten opportunities you'll want to know about...").

• Choose the best times for the congregation to stand and sit—avoid the "up and down" syndrome.

• Use lighting to enhance the most important worship element going on at any given time. (Be sure to transition smoothly between elements.)

• Advise any stage participants on the best times to approach or leave the stage so they don't distract or create dead spots.

• Instead of saying, "We have a *video*," or "We have a *video* of that story," say, "Let's watch that story together," or "Check out what one mission group was able to do."

• Fade the audio out of the end of a movie clip, but leave the video on the screen as "live" music begins. (This is very effective!)

• Encourage the band to work through transitions ahead of time so that the musical flow is not interrupted.

• Tie the words spoken for the communion celebration into the overall theme of the worship service.

• Play a bit of appropriate music to set up and "bookend" a drama.

• Play soft music under prayers to soften hearts.

Here's the deal—integration is *free*! It costs *nothing* in dollars and cents. You can begin integrating your pieces this week! Small churches and large churches all have equal ability to integrate their worship, and it makes *all* the difference in the world.

PARTICIPATION OVERCOMING PERFORMANCE

As we moved into the new millennium, we noticed that the ground was shifting beneath our worship paradigm. We realized our people had a greater need to *belong* than to be struck by our stage work. *All* people are on a search to be accepted, a quest to know that their thoughts, opinions, actions, service, experiences, and lives are important and useful. People need to know that we care before they will care what we know about rolling out great music, media, or even terrific messages.

As a result, we've made a 180-degree turn as we've worked to increase opportunities for overall participation in the worship celebrations. Here are some examples of what a pastor or worship host might say to make worship more participatory.

- "Turn to the person next to you and share an experience you've had with…"
- "Let's say this prayer out loud together as it comes up on the screen."
- "Let's stand to worship in song, and on your way up, greet someone and tell them how great it is to see them here today."
- "Stand up and say the name of the person who first exposed you to Jesus."
- "Speak out loud the first name of someone who needs our prayers today."

When time is limited, invitations like these provide an opportunity for everyone to participate simultaneously. When we have a little more time in the service, we invite people to pray or talk together in small groups. We *never* used to do this in the days of the megachurch movement, but now we're seeing that postmodern people are wanting it, needing it, and responding very well to it even if at first it doesn't feel natural. It's like taking medicine. You hate it going down, but afterward you feel so much better! People may need a little help breaking out of their shells, but when they do, they feel so glad that they've connected. Although we're a large church, during these discussion and prayer times we do our best to make sure that everyone is included.

Small churches have the edge on the participation piece. It's much easier to engage a smaller group of people in worship and community. Larger churches may be tempted to ride on performance, but a one-way worship conversation cannot engage people over the long haul. In any size church, we must make an intentional effort to reach out and make worship personal, to see the congregation not as one large mass of humanity, but as unique individuals coming to find health and life in Jesus. The rewards are great when we allow participation to overcome performance.

> In any size church, we must make an intentional effort to reach out and make worship personal, to see the congregation not as one large mass of humanity, but as unique individuals coming to find health and life in Jesus.

Endnote

1. For more examples of creative ways to open a celebration, check out Kim Miller's *Handbook for Multisensory Worship*, volumes I and II (Nashville, TN: Abingdon Press, 1999, 2001).

CHAPTER 14

Powerful Prayers for Everyday People

"That's the kind of people the Father is out looking for: those who are simply and honestly themselves before him in their worship."

JOHN 4:23, THE MESSAGE

rayer is two-way communication with God. Inside every celebration we are sure to hear a word *from* God. We traditionally call this the *message* or the *sermon*. In multisensory worship, we often enhance this word with a video story, a song (poetry of the culture), a well-planned live interview, or even a drama of some sort. No matter how we've heard *from* God, however, we always create a time to talk back *to* God. These prayers can take on myriad forms, as imaginative as our minds can allow.

As worship designers, we must place ourselves in the hearts and lives of the worshippers. With wisdom and compassion, we are called to give oral framing to what participants might desire to say to God in response to what they've experienced in worship. As we seek to guide the practice of prayer in worship, we must prepare well (perhaps by spending time in prayer ourselves), knowing that participants may need help articulating what is in their hearts and minds.

Prayer is simply talking to God, and prayer in worship is simply talking to God on behalf of the gathered faith community. On the following pages, you'll find examples of prayers we've used in our worship celebrations. Some were written for holidays or particular occasions. Others are simply "everyday prayers," suitable for any worship service. While you may use these prayers in your worship, the most powerful prayers will be the ones *you* write—prayers created and spoken from the heart God has given you for your people... amen.

Theme:

Pursuing the Dream

Occasion: Martin Luther King Jr. weekend

Desired Outcome: Participants will become part of the authentic community that will relentlessly pursue the dream of a multicultural kingdom.

Background: At the close of the message, three worship participants (a diverse trio) led this prayer together:

LEADER: "We know God has called us to demonstrate the multicultural kingdom…and we know we're not there yet. God is calling us to pursue the dream harder than ever, whatever the cost. Let's stand together to say this prayer of intention as it appears on the screen."

Prayer:

We have a dream…
To be a faith community that fully demonstrates the call of Jesus
Where people of all ages, gender, culture,
All backgrounds and economic status are welcomed;
Where God's love breaks down the wall of racial barriers,
Personal preferences, and preconceived notions about others.
Where we lay down our pride and prejudice,
Our fear of difference and our burden of sin.
And where we fully demonstrate the
Unnatural, unconditional, and undeniable love of God.
Together we say, "Thy kingdom come,
Thy will be done on earth as it is in heaven."
This is our dream. Amen.

Theme:

One Heart and Soul

Occasion: Any

Desired Outcome: Participants will realize the full presence and blessing of God that come only through community.

Background: As preparation for a message in a series on Authentic Community, we led this time of participation and prayer.

HOST: "We all face the same challenge...to find a community of people we truly like, who feel safe and inviting, who will faithfully draw us closer to God. We all have fears and anxieties about meeting people and connecting into community. I know I do! But ultimately, most of us wouldn't be here today if we didn't want the full presence of God in our lives.

"What brought you to this place of community, and what keeps you here? Love? Jesus? Spirit? Music? Truth?" (Ask for out-loud, one-word responses from the congregation. It helps to make them comfortable responding.)

"Thanks for your response. Psalm 133 says, 'How good and pleasant it is when brothers [and sisters] dwell together in unity...For there the Lord bestows his blessing, even life forevermore.' Let's pray this prayer together as it appears on the screen."

Prayer:

Lord, we've come for a variety of
    reasons.
To find hope and healing,
To give our kids hope and
    direction,
To discover a place of love and
    acceptance,
And to live out your call on our lives.
Today we ask for courage and
    strength

To reach out beyond ourselves
In order to truly become part of
    the kingdom of God,
The authentic community.
Most of all, today we want
To give you honor and glory
By giving you all of who we are.
We give you our hearts and our souls.
Have your way in our lives, Jesus.
    Amen.

Powerful Prayers for Everyday People

Theme:

Resurrection—Alive Again!

Occasion: Easter

Desired Outcome: Participants will stand up and move forward in the power of the Resurrection.

Background: Easter brings lots of guests to worship celebrations. We designed a celebration of hope, careful to include some pieces that might feel familiar to the guests. For our prayer aloud together, we said the Lord's Prayer. People seem to truly appreciate and feel more at home when they can genuinely participate.

Later, after viewing Mike Martindale's "resurrection story,"[1] we asked Mike to come up to the stage. In each service, the congregation gave him a standing ovation. I then told Mike how much he and his story meant to us, and invited him to pray. It was such a powerful moment, and something that Mike could do for us and with us. Here is the prayer we wrote for Mike to speak:

Prayer:
Lord, thank you for new life.
Thank you for each day we share.
Thank you for your amazing love
That is shown through all creation,
And through the people you've put in
    our lives.
This day belongs to you,
And we give you all the honor and
    glory. Amen.

Theme:

The Best Godly Man Show, Period

Occasion: Father's Day weekend

Desired Outcome: Male participants will actively take their places
as men of God. Female participants will support them as they
take this step of faith.

Background: We did this entire
celebration in the style of the popular cable TV sports show with a
similar title. Leather couches, coffee cups, and men sitting on the
couches discussing the challenges
of being Christlike men, hus-
bands, and dads. Our pastor led

the discussion and then, at the close of this creative celebration, asked all the
men in the room to stand and say this prayer of promise out loud together as
it appeared on the screen.

Prayer:

Father God, we stand before you today,
Challenged to take our place as men of God,
Passionate in our pursuit of you.
We confess to allowing ourselves to be tamed,
Forgetting the mission that you have called us
To take on as your disciples.
Hear our prayer as we seek the strength
To flee distraction, to pursue integrity,
To fight the good fight, to take hold of your call on our lives
And the lives of those we love.
This we ask because of you,
Our mighty God, our passionate Father.
In Jesus' name, amen.

Theme:

Dad Almighty

Occasion: Father's Day, any

Desired Outcome: Participants will embrace and enjoy the love of their heavenly Father.

Romans 8:15-16

DadALMIGHTY

Background: Normally, we've used video clips from movies to introduce an entire worship celebration or to make a point within the message. Todd wanted to use a video clip from the movie *Smoke Signals* that didn't seem to fit in either place, but when I saw it, I realized it would set up the prayer in a powerful way. The clip is simply video footage of a huge river flowing vigorously between rock and mountain formations. The voiceover is a man, reflecting on his own father experience. "Shall we forgive our fathers?" he starts out, then continues with a monologue that would catch the heart of any adult.

Coming out of that clip (with soft, live piano music in the background), I spoke these words to our people:

"Shall we forgive our fathers? How shall we understand a heavenly Father who seeks to love, discipline, and give generously to each of his children every day? Is our understanding of Dad Almighty totally dependent on our experience of Dad-so-earthly—our human fathers?

"The truth today for all of us is that, yes, we must forgive. For if we never understand and receive the love and amazing grace of this heavenly Father, we can never be truly transformed in Christ. We will at best be lost children, gazing longingly through the glass at others who have learned the love and acceptance of Dad Almighty, yet settling for never knowing it ourselves. We go about our lives pretending to be loved, but not truly knowing and feeling it on the inside. Will you bow your heads and pray with me now?"

HOST *(praying):* "Forgive us, Father, for we've tried to live our lives by numbly assenting to faith, rather than courageously renewing our minds with the acceptance and assurance of the powerful love you have for each one of us. 'How great is the love the Father has lavished on us, that we should be called the children of God,' your children. May our time with you today change our hearts and minds toward renewal and health. Amen."

Theme:

Spirit of Faith

Occasion: Bikers for Jesus weekend (special event)

Desired Outcome: Participants will move out of their zones of comfort to live with a pioneering, risk-taking spirit.

Background: Recently we discovered the power of motorcycles! We have a Bikers for Jesus group at Ginghamsburg, and we decided we would host a bikers outreach event. We invited motorcyclists from all over to come for worship and to receive a "Blessing of the Bikes" from our pastor (complete with a splash of water!). We discovered that bikers are passionate about their lifestyle and hobby, and that there is a definite spiritual connection that can be captured through such an event. Here is the blessing we said during the outdoor event after the worship celebration. ("Laying hands" on each of the bikes is important.)

Blessing of the Bikes:
May the road ahead be safe,
May all your turns be smooth,
May your feet always find solid
     ground,
And may the spirit of faith always
     ride with you.
Go with God's wind. Amen.

Endnote

1. Mike Martindale suffered a stroke and survived a three-month coma after an accident on a three-wheeler. His story is included on the accompanying DVD.

CHAPTER 15

A Mission-Driven Messenger

"The man who follows the crowd will usually get no further than the crowd.

The man who walks alone is likely to find himself in places no one has ever been."

ALAN ASHLEY-PITT

Isn't it fascinating that throughout the centuries of Christendom, the spoken word has remained the single, most powerful form of persuading men and women of the truth about Jesus Christ? While God uses many creative art forms to enhance and enrich the message, we still need to hear someone convince us of the truth through the spoken word.

Jesus had a powerful gift of persuasion. People followed him into the countryside with no promise of lunch. They thronged into homes to hear what he had to say. Seekers were known to lower friends through roofs, reach out to grab at Jesus' garment, and even climb trees just to see and hear him. Luke 4:32 says, "They were amazed at his teaching, because his message had authority."

Deep down, we all want to be changed—to have our hurts healed and our issues resolved. Perhaps that is why we still listen for the voice of God in the moments of the weekend message. We long for a message that will move our hearts and change our lives.

Mike Slaughter is a speaker who is passionate about communicating powerful truth through the spoken word. I interviewed him to hear his take on how messages can move hearts.

SERVANT INTERVIEW
Mike Slaughter

KIM: *Mike, you always come to the design team meeting on Wednesdays prepared with a "word" for the upcoming weekend. When do you know that you have the right word for the congregation in any given week? How are you sure?*

MIKE: It has to be a word for me first, something that speaks to me in my life. The thing that I struggle with in my heart is what other people struggle with in their hearts. It's connected to passion. If you're not passionate about it, other people will never be passionate. Many messages and worship experiences are lifeless because they lack passion. Passion isn't something you can prepare or even train; it comes from within. It's very much a spiritual thing. As the Spirit touches my spirit, it ignites my passion. It then becomes something I can be contagious about with people. The word has to come from passion.

KIM: *At times I've observed that there is something inside of you that doesn't feel quite right, and it becomes a motivation for a message or a word to the congregation. How does God direct your angst, the urgency inside you?*

MIKE: Angst and urgency go together. Yesterday I was reading in the *Transformation Journal* [a daily devotional tool written by Ginghamsburg's Discipleship Team, available via the e-store at www.ginghamsburg.org]. It spoke about how we are stewards of the mysteries of God. Those mysteries have to be fleshed out for people to understand, because they're not going to understand them or study them to the degree that the leader of the church will. Urgency creates the incarnation of the Word. You become passionate about the truth, but then it has to be incarnated or made less complicated before people can get it and incorporate it into their lives. Then people can become passionate about it.

KIM: *So you'll read a word in your daily time with God, then you start to think, "How can I explain this to the congregation in a way that they truly get it?"*

MIKE: If it ignites my passion and spirit, yes. This week we're studying about "Jesus and Witness" in our *Transformation Journal*. The magazine Fast Company recently had an article that spoke about budget and something I saw as related to witness. It said that what some small companies do is create "buzz" with their people, and those people are the ones out there selling it—the customers. They're not talking about leader-type people; it's the B-type people that create the buzz. Once you ignite the passion in people, it creates a buzz in them and makes them infectious and contagious. That's witness. The angst and urgency is to connect these truths to people's passion so that they are then applying the word.

This week the passion for me is about that small window of opportunity that parents have to truly affect their children with the gospel so that their children are radical. I want parents to teach their children not just to become believers who attend church, act morally, and pay their tithe, but to be infectious Christians so that their very lives, no matter what they do, are driven by the gospel for Jesus Christ.

KIM: *What important learnings about leading a church have surfaced for you in the last two years?*

MIKE: One of the biggest things is that everyone keeps studying about generations and how they are alike, how they are different, and how it affects the church. There is an ancient truth that the gospel is going to hold for every generation.

Businesses, in this whole postmodern movement, are discovering that in many ways they have gotten too complex and have now gone into a back-to-basics movement. Businesses are asking, "Who is our primary customer?" I've been in a back-to-basics movement in the last two years. We're in the core business of making radical disciples of Jesus Christ. In the church growth movement, it became really complex. We got into all kind of businesses—bookstores, coffee shops. While I'm not discounting the value of some of that, I'm saying that we can forget or get distracted from our primary business, which is making disciples of Jesus Christ.

KIM: *How have your learnings come through in your teaching and preaching?*

MIKE: The key to any movement is a leader translating what God is teaching so that people can apply it. Many of my messages teach the importance of being in community. It is critical for living a life that is formed by the Word. We want everyone to be in a cell group. We want everyone in the next four years to experience mission somewhere in the world. We are giving people back-to-basics applications and naming the path of discipleship.

In our attempt to reach a nonlinear world, we can't eliminate some important linear steps. As children develop, they do so in a linear way. They have to crawl before they walk or run. Linear is part of development and is unchanging. Every generation is unique and linear at the same time.

KIM: *Let's talk about worship for a few moments. What do you feel makes a* *powerful worship experience? What are the ingredients?*

MIKE: Obviously, there must be a realization of Christ and the Holy Spirit. People must realize that "where two or three are gathered" makes it holy space, no matter where you are, because of the presence of Christ. What makes great worship is the realization that people aren't just there singing and listening to a word, but recognizing that they are in the presence of Christ in a unique way. Worshipping in community creates something that you can't quite experience by yourself. In worship, it's vital that we find ways for everyone to truly participate. Worship is always centered on the integrity of the word of God.

KIM: *How does the message that you preach play into the overall picture of a powerful worship experience?*

MIKE: The whole worship experience at Ginghamsburg is built around the message, beginning with the word. For us, we think about the music, theme, and metaphor based on the word. It's the interaction of all of these elements together.

KIM: *What did you learn in seminary that you still hold with you that is absolutely essential to every message?*

MIKE: That Jesus never spoke without a parable. Great preaching is picture painting, so storytelling is critical to preaching. I also learned to always be true to the intent of the Word and to not manipulate the Word.

KIM: *What were you taught in seminary that you needed to unlearn?*

MIKE: I needed to unlearn the nonteam approach to worship preparation, where the messages and worship experiences were developed apart from each other—solo preparation verses team preparation.

KIM: *Where do you go for creative input and inspiration?*

MIKE: I look to my D.R.I.V.E. acronym.[1]
  • *D*evotion to God
  • *R*eadiness/Reading for lifelong learning
  • *I*nvesting in key relationships
  • *V*isioning for the future
  • *E*xercise

Take today for instance. I've done my devotion time. My reading was the Fast Company article about buzz, which was about the idea of witnessing, in addition to the *Transformation Journal* Scriptures. I've networked with other people who I think

> What makes great worship is the realization that people aren't just there singing and listening to a word, but recognizing that they are in the presence of Christ in a unique way.

are world-changers in how they lead their churches. That's part of invest-
ing in key relationships and visioning. Networking with creative, anointed
people who understand the times is critical. A lot of folks network with the
wrong people. If you're going to get ahead, you have to network with the
right people. I don't mean "getting ahead" in a worldly sense of what it
means to advance. I'm talking about being a part of the progressive movement of God using the gifts that God's given you for kingdom use. Lastly, I
exercise daily.

KIM: *Your exercise program has gone beyond being a simple piece of your day to
actually being a demonstrated metaphor for life. You've experienced transformation in a physical way that has given you insight about what spiritual
transformation truly entails. It has greatly influenced our congregation on a
physical and spiritual level as well.*

*Is there anything else that you would want to say to pastors and worship
planners?*

MIKE: One of the keys to any worship experience is moving forward in obedience to God with the fear of God, not the fear of people. Worship loses
the prophetic voice of God when we fear people and not God. In another
sense, we must remember that unless worship is incarnated and makes
sense to the people who are participating, it's ineffective. You have to do
worship based on truth and the fear of God—a healthy fear of God. You
must have a *passion* to connect people using both things together.

KIM: *Thanks, Mike. As always, it's great to be in team with you.*

When we design worship, we incorporate art forms of all types, including
media, drama, music, and artistic metaphor. The *truth* of God's word, however, is always the catalyst for moving hearts and transforming lives. Praise be
to God for the incredible message we've been given through the Word.

Endnote

1. The D.R.I.V.E. acronym is taken from a message series delivered in January and
   February 2002. These messages can be viewed on Ginghamsburg's Web site,
   www.ginghamsburg.org.

A Ministry of Mud 'n' Spit

> "Having said this, he spit on the ground, made some mud
> with the saliva, and put it on the man's eyes. 'Go,' he
> told him, 'wash in the Pool of Siloam.' So the man went
> and washed, and came home seeing" (John 9:6-7).

What does it take to make a miracle happen? From our own limited perspectives, we imagine God with sparkling magic potions carefully arranged in a glittering heavenly toolbox. Maybe with a few wands thrown in for the really tough jobs.

God's best work, however, has always been done with amazingly ordinary stuff—water, mud, spit, a piece of stale bread, a barn, a teenage girl, twelve dysfunctional disciples. God uses ordinary objects in regular places with everyday people. The good news for every single worship designer on the planet is that miracles happen when the divine intersects with the ordinary.

The metaphor I use for my life is "mud and spit." I'm fascinated with the four Gospels and the earthiness of everything Jesus did. If Jesus were walking on earth today, in our time, I don't know how he would heal the blind man. Maybe instead of using mud and spit, he would use some thick espresso or aromatic candle wax. On that particular day, however, Jesus spat in the dust, made a clay paste with his saliva, rubbed the paste onto the blind guy's eyes—then told the guy to go wash in a pool. That's creativity. That's using what you have, where you have it, and whom you have it with—I love that! Stories like that give me hope that I can do this too. I'm an everyday person. I've been touched by heaven—empowered by God. I can use what God's already put in me and around me—just ordinary stuff—and begin to change the world.

Designing worship is a ministry of mud and spit. God wants each and every worship designer to know that with God's Spirit, we are uniquely gifted to be a part of making miracles happen. We're everyday people using ordinary objects in regular places to create powerful moments in which others have the opportunity to experience God.

As I bring this writing to a close, here is your very first assignment for designing worship, straight from a little yellow sticky note next to my computer:

- Care more than others think wise.
- Risk more than others think safe.
- Dream more than others think practical.
- Expect more than others think possible.

Amen.

Sample Scripts for Worship Celebrations

Great Expectations

Biblical Story: Zechariah's Dilemma, adapted from Luke 1:5-24

Actors: One storyteller (Story can be read from a script.)

Costume: None

Set: None

Suggested Song: "I Can't Fight This Feeling Anymore" (REO Speedwagon) (It is not necessary to obtain permission to use this music if it's performed live in a worship celebration.)

Description: Storyteller is seated on stage, lit separately from the band if possible. On-screen, show hand-drawn or scanned illustrations of the Bible story. After the storyteller finishes each section, resume the song.

Perform the first verse of the song vocally, then play a soft, instrumental version under the storytelling.

STORYTELLER: During the rule of Herod, King of Judea, there was a priest in the regiment of Abijah whose name was Zechariah. His wife was named Elizabeth. Together they lived honorably before God, careful to keep the commandments and enjoying a clear conscience before God, but they were childless because Elizabeth could never conceive, and now they were quite old.

It so happened that while Zechariah was carrying out his priestly duties before God, he was chosen to enter the sanctuary of God and burn incense. The congregation was gathered and praying outside the Temple at that hour. Unannounced, an angel of God appeared next to the altar of incense. Zechariah was paralyzed in fear. But the angel assured him, "Your prayer has been heard. Elizabeth, your wife, will bear a son by you. You are to name him John."

Sing the second verse of the song, then play soft, instrumental music under the storytelling.

STORYTELLER: "You're going to leap for joy, Zechariah," the angel spoke, "and not only you, but many will delight in John's birth. He'll achieve great stature with God. He'll be filled with the Holy Spirit from the moment he's born. He will turn many sons and daughters of Israel back to their God. He will herald God's arrival in the style and strength of Elijah, soften the hearts of parents to children, and kindle understanding among hardened skeptics; he'll get the people ready for the Messiah."

Sing the song's third and fourth verses, then play soft, instrumental music under the storytelling.

STORYTELLER: Zechariah said to the angel, "Do you expect me to believe this? I'm an old man and my wife is an old woman." But the angel said, "I am Gabriel, sent by God, sent especially to bring you this news. But because you won't believe, you'll be unable to speak a word until the day of your son's birth. Every word I've spoken to you will come true on time...God's time."

Meanwhile, the congregation waiting for Zechariah was getting restless, wondering what was keeping him so long in the sanctuary. When he came out and couldn't speak, they knew he had seen a vision. Zechariah continued speechless and had to use sign language with the people.

When the course of his priestly assignment was completed, Zechariah went back home. It wasn't long before his wife, Elizabeth, conceived.

Resume song and play to the end.

Sample Scripts for Worship Celebrations

Aim High

Biblical Story: David (from 1 Samuel 16:1-17)

Actors: Two males, one age ten to thirteen and one age twenty to thirty. Their appearances should be similar enough to convey a younger and older version of a single individual.

Costume: Both males wear identical costumes: jeans with holes, a white T-shirt, and the same bandana. Both are barefoot and have slingshots with a rock.

Set: Large rock(s) to give the ambience of a shepherd's space

Suggested Song: "Man After Your Own Heart" (Wayne Kirkpatrick and Billy Sprague, performed by Gary Chapman) (Music must be obtained separately.)

Description: This is a two-part drama. The first monologue begins during the instrumental introduction. The younger David is seated on a rock. He begins talking as the lights go up. He is confident and passionate. As the vocalists sing two verses, the older David approaches the set. He walks slowly, and the two Davids pass each other as the young David leaves the stage. The older David delivers his monologue, then exits after the lights go dark. After he leaves, the vocalist finishes the song.

At the designated points in the song, pause the vocals, and have the actors deliver their monologues. Continue to play soft instrumental music under the actors' spoken words. After each monologue, resume the song.

MONOLOGUE 1 *(Younger David)*

A young boy is seated on a rock. He is a bit cocky and outspoken and is fooling around with a slingshot. He begins talking as lights go up. *(Lights up.)*

Play the instrumental introduction. Monologue 1 is spoken over music.

YOUNGER DAVID: Hi. My name's Davey. Nobody really calls me David much…'cept my old man…when he's mad. *(Getting more excited.)* Have you ever shot a rock from a slingshot? I have. *(Standing.)* I could hit that light up there *(pointing up)* and break it in a million pieces. I could nail one right between your eyes…if I ever needed to, which I don't. *(Sits back down.)*

Mostly what I do is kill animals. My dad owns some sheep, and they couldn't defend themselves if their lives depended on it, which they do.

So I go after the lions and the bears. *(Looking at the audience.)* You don't believe me, but I do. When you're out in the hills, you get a lot of time to practice. Here's what I say every time I'm up against a bear. *(Standing.)* "God, I love you with everything I have, and today there is nothing we can't do together." And then I just go for it...aim high. *(Lights blackout.)*

Continue the song through the first two verses as older David approaches. Then play soft, instrumental music under monologue.

MONOLOGUE 2 *(Older David)*

A young man is seated on a rock. His personality is confident and passionate. He holds a slingshot. He begins talking as the lights go up. *(Lights up as David begins to speak.)*

OLDER DAVID: Name's David. You might know me for a lot of things, but I need to tell you firsthand what happened with the "Goliath Project."

I was always the "runt of the litter," as you would say. The youngest of eight sons of my old man, Jesse. I don't have to tell you I got the bad end of everything. The older ones always got the best jobs while I was left looking after our sorry little sheep. They got to go fight when I stayed back.

But it wasn't all bad. I learned about the companionship of God—yep, God. Ever since I was young, I've been preoccupied with the unseen Presence. It was God who taught me to just stand and aim high. I'm a straight shot with a reckless passion. Cocky, too. I'd learned to hunt down lions and bears. But after a while I found myself going after the heart of my God.

Oh, and I am a little crazy, too. So when I catch a look at this jerk, Goliath, who dares to defy the army of my God, I tell them all that it's going to be OK. It's God's battle, and I can nail this guy right between the eyes. Well, God and I. Yeah. Aim high. *(Lights blackout, older David exits.)*

Resume song and play to the end.

Every Day

Theme: Devotion to God

Actors: Three readers, ages eighteen to twenty-eight (Try to vary gender and race.)

Costume: Casual dress in appropriate Gen-X style

Set: Three stools that can be lit separately from the band

Song: "Everyday" (Dave Matthews Band) (Music must be obtained separately.)

Description: Reader's theater with three readers. Reader one is a skeptical resolution maker, reader two is overly optimistic and materialistic, and reader three is more tuned into devotion to God. All are oblivious of one another. When saying their lines, it appears that each is making a list of New Year's resolutions, equipped with a notebook and pen.

As each reader finishes his or her line, the next reader says the same word at the same time to lead into his or her next line. Overlapping words are indicated by italics in the script. The entire piece is spoken in two "pockets" at appropriate breaks in the Dave Matthews song "Everyday." Breaks should be timed at the discretion of the band leader, with instrumental music continuing softly under the readers.

Begin the song. When the band leader breaks, begin the following dialogue.

READER 1: Let's see…January 200__. I can't believe it. Better put down some resolutions before this year gets away from me. *Number one…*

READER 2: *Number one…*lose ten pounds. That's how much I think I gained over *Christmas.*

READER 1: *Christmas* was so fattening! I better start exercising! I hate to think about it, but hey, no time like the *present.*

READER 3: *Presence.* I need the presence of God in my life every day. Here I am, Lord. I'm not gonna let go of you *this year.*

READER 1: *This year* should be the year for my new job. I hate just going through the motions week in and week out. I hereby make a resolution to find something I can really sink my teeth into *every day.*

READER 3: *Every day* will be a new day with you, Jesus. Part of not letting go of you is my promise to be more honest with you. I need someone who can listen to *everything,* who understands *my struggles.*

READER 2: *My struggle* is with that old piece of junk I'm driving. A car. This is the year of the car! I'm thinking the new Audi TT! *Yes!*

READER 3: *Yes!* Because, Jesus, if I can't be totally real with you, well, what good is our relationship? And I want to know the real "you."

Resume music. Break at band leader's discretion. Readers continue.

READER 2: Blue. My new car will be blue. This is gonna be a great *year!*

READER 1: *Years* come and go. I'm twenty-three, for heaven's sake. I'm going to finally map out that five-year plan that my dad always told me I needed. Should that be a today thing? *Oh Lord...*

READER 3: *O Lord,* if I spend time with you every day, would I...do you think I could "hear" from you? Do you give directions to people? Plans, ideas? *Dreams?*

READER 2: *Dreams* are what life is made of. I'm dreaming of a green New Year (if you know what *I mean*).

READER 1: *I mean,* it's crazy to think I can keep my resolutions. It's never happened before! Even if I do apply for a better job, there's no guarantee I would be able to *get it.*

READER 3: *Get it*! I get it! I'll meet you here, Lord, *every day*!

READER 2: *Every day* I'm gonna go for it. The car, the dream, the money— *every day.*

READER 1: *Every day.* Oh Lord, I can't believe I'll have to pull my life together again every single morning,

ALL: Every day!

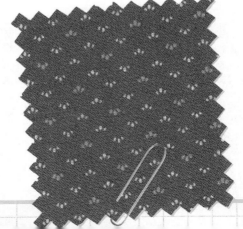

Generopoly—
The Game of Generous Giving

Actors: Two young men and two young women

Costume: Casual dress.

Set: A game table and four chairs. On the table is a game of "Generopoly," four bottles of soda, and any other props appropriate to "game night."

Description: The band begins by singing "If I Had a Million Dollars." Two young men and two young women approach the stage, talking and laughing in muted tones, then settle in on the set at the table. *(Low lights up on drama)*. The players continue to set up the game, occasionally singing along with the band.

The band finishes the song. (Lights up on drama, down on band.)

BJ: *(to band)* We'll take it from here, guys. If I had a million dollars…

TERRI: If *I* had a million dollars...

CARL: No, if *I* had a million dollars...

ABBY: What? What would you do with it?

CARL: Well, let's just say I wouldn't be sitting here gearing up for another night of classic Monopoly.

ABBY: *(holding up the lid like Vanna White)* Not Monopoly, Carl, Generopoly—The Game of Generous Giving.

CARL: What's that about?

TERRI: It probably wouldn't hurt you to find out.

CARL: I can play that game…bring it on!

BJ: Might not be as easy as you think, big guy.

ABBY: I think it depends on what kind of person you are…

TERRI: Take your turn—you're first.

CARL: OK, OK. *(He rolls and quickly moves to the space marked "Income Tithe," counting one-two-three-four)* Income Tax…no, wait…"Income *Tithe*. Pay 10 percent or $200.00." Can somebody tell me what "Income Tithe" is?

ABBY: Tithe means 10 percent. You give 10 percent of your income.

CARL: You mean just…give?

ABBY: Yeah…give. Give up, like to God. You give God 10 percent or so, and God takes care of everything else you need. *Comprende?*

CARL: *(sarcastically)* Oh, that's great.

BJ: I don't get it.

TERRI: Well, it *is* Generopoly. See what the card says? "Seek first the king-dom of God and all the rest will be given to you."

CARL: So you're saying I could still win?

ABBY: Sure you could. Let's keep going. Terri.

TERRI: OK, sure. I'll just hop on down the neighborhood here...*(rolls and counts)* St. Charles Place...I'll take it! Sounds like a great street for a single-parent housing unit.

CARL: Single-parent housing unit...have I missed something here?

ABBY: Maybe that this game is about giving, not getting.

TERRI: That's always been a hard concept for Carl to grasp.

CARL: Hey!

TERRI: Sorry.

BJ: *(rolling)* This is my lucky day...I can just feel it *(rolls and moves to Community Chest)*. Oh cool, Community Chest!

ABBY: Not Community Chest, BJ. Treasure Chest. It's called "Treasure Chest" in this game. Pick up the card.

BJ: *(picking up the card)* Hmm..."You just opened a shelter for the homeless, and you'll need to buy food. Collect $150.00."

CARL: What?

BJ: Hey, I'm getting it now. It's Generopoly! Read the fine print on the card: "For where your treasure is, there will your heart be also." I like this game!

CARL: It isn't making a lot of sense...it seems backward.

ABBY: My turn *(grabbing the dice)*. I've got a great feeling here *(rolls, moves, and picks up card)*. Chance: "Congratulations! You used your vacation to build a home at a project in Mississippi. Advance to the nearest railroad, and it's yours for your next trip."

CARL: This is ridiculous. I'm sitting here competing with Mother Teresa on the Reading Railroad, the Pope's feeding the hungry, and the church lady here is putting up single-parent housing in place of red hotels. Give me those dice. *(He rolls and moves.)* Treasure Chest. Hmm...maybe I'll get lucky, I need a break. *(He reads the card.)* "When given the opportunity to sponsor a needy child at church, you kept the money and purchased five Big Macs instead. Go to jail. Go directly to jail. Do not pass Go..."

All: "Do not collect $200.00."

CARL: Thanks, everybody.

All: No problem! *(ad lib)*

CARL: Then again, maybe I *do* have a problem.

BJ: Admitting it is always the first step toward recovery. What is the problem you speak of?

CARL: I can't seem to get this. It seems rigged or something. You can't get ahead in this game without giving something away. It's just not natural for me…I don't think that way.

TERRI: But you should…*(Carl glares at her.)* could! I mean, you could. You can learn generous giving.

ABBY: Terri's right. It's a whole different way of living.

BJ: Think of it as making a Boardwalk salary…but choosing a Baltic Avenue lifestyle.

CARL: Oooh…that hurts.

TERRI: 'Cause no one can serve two masters.

ABBY: Even if he does have a million dollars!

(Lights blackout.)

(Band reprises "If I Had a Million Dollars")

Socks Knocks:
A Call to Worship Story

The sun did not shine; it was too wet to play.
So we sat in the house all that cold, cold day.
I sat there with Susie; we sat there, we two.
And I said, "It looks to me like we've nothing to do."

Too wet to go out and too cold to play ball.
So we sat in the house; we did nothing at all.
So all that we did was sit! sit! sit! sit!
And we did not like it, not one little bit.

And then, something went bump!
How that bump made us jump!
We looked, then we saw him outside on the mat.
We looked and we saw him, this little black cat.

We looked at that cat mewing outside the door.
We knew Dad would say, "This cat is no more.
No more can this cat be inside of our house,
Than a dog or a bird or a horse or a mouse.

For cats are not good, and houses need locks.
And no one who lives here will answer their knocks."
Because even if cats are cute like a fox,
Even if cats have white feet just like Socks,

And even if cats call and ask to come in,
You just can't give up and feed them and then...
Wish that you hadn't, for Dad says, "You know...
That cat's too much trouble; that cat's got to go!"

Now why, you may ask, tell this tale here in church?
"Please," you are saying, "Get us out of this lurch!"
For cats are not bad, and dads not all mean.
And so what is the point that remains to be seen?

I'll tell you now...
Jesus the Savior calls from outside the door,
"Listen to me, I'm asking for more.
I'm asking for you to let me come in,
To come live with you, to clean out the sin.

"I want to live now in this house here with you.
I want to share all of the things that you do."
Behold, the Lord Jesus stands there and knocks.
Not unlike the cat, whose name was called Socks.
But grown-ups, their lives full of sin! sin! sin! sin!
Can close themselves up, and not let him come in.

So today is a call to listen to him,
To open the door of your life full of sin,
To ask him to come in, and eat with you too,
'Cause life with this Jesus is all up to *you*!

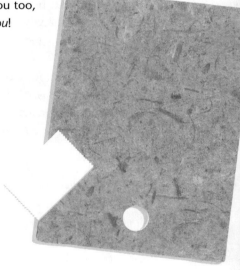

We Danced Anyway

Word: "We know that in all things God works for the good of those who love him, who have been called according to his purpose" (Romans 8:28). 1 Thessalonians 5:18; Psalm 30

Felt Need: I don't understand how to "dance" (be thankful) when my world is falling apart.

Desired Outcome: Participants will choose to "dance" anyway, unleashing God's strength and power.

Theme: We Danced Anyway

Look: Ballet Dancer

Play video clip from Hope Floats *(scene that begins with Sandra Bullock speaking to her father, then they begin dancing).*

Begin live music while the characters in the video are dancing. Fade video clip and bring up live music (band and vocalist), "We Danced Anyway."

OPENING WORDS:

Someone once said that life is what *really* happens on the way to your dreams. In other words, things don't always go as we plan them...

Parents grow old.

Relationships get broken.

Children go a different way.

Life can become painful, and you and I forget to dance.

Today is going to be a different kind of experience. There are great stories of faith in this room, and today we are going to teach one another about faith, about true thanksgiving, and about dancing through tough times. Today is the story of a God who calls us to give thanks no matter what happens...

even when it's not our plan,

even when it hurts,

even when it doesn't make sense, and

even when we don't understand the words.

God invites us to dance anyway and teaches us the steps.

Today we hear the stories of real people who have felt the blow of real pain, who've cried a multitude of tears, and yet, through it all, have learned to dance anyway.

Today is your story too. Whatever is going on in each of our lives, we need to step out and begin to dance, saying, "Thank you, God. We trust you no matter what. And even though we don't always 'understand the words,' we open ourselves to your presence and power in our lives, through our tears and in our pain. *We dance anyway.*

Play video or invite live speakers to share their stories. After the stories, have the worship leader lead congregation members in praying for each other as the band plays softly. At the end of the prayer time, continue with the worship celebration. Suggested additional songs include "I Need You" by LeAnn Rimes (to be sung as the offering is collected), "The Dance" by Garth Brooks, and "I Hope You Dance" by Lee Ann Womack.

Invite additional speakers to share their stories. The story we used at Ginghamsburg follows below. Have a keyboardist provide soft piano music in the background as the speaker tells his or her story.

SPEAKER: On May 25, 1995, we lost a child. Lydia was eighty-six days old when her heart stopped. We knew there were problems with her heart and were anticipating surgery to repair the abnormalities. She had just begun smiling and was fascinated with her hands. Although I knew she was ill, I was devastated when she was suddenly gone. How could I get through the day? Life changed instantly for us. Many people avoided us because they didn't know what to say. Others said the wrong things. The honest truth is there is little to say in the face of a tragedy like losing a child. Initially, nothing could replace our lost child, comfort our grief, or fill the hole in our hearts.

I want to wear a T-shirt that says, "Be nice to me; my child just died." I find myself short-tempered, humorless, and impatient...just dancing the dance. I went to a party, and a young couple was there with their first-born, a beautiful, blue-eyed butterball. I found out her name was Lydia and she was born three weeks after my Lydia. Will I ever be able to look at her without seeing what my little girl could have been?

Dancing the dance. I bravely drove to the hospital where Lydia spent several weeks in intensive care. Though painful, I walked through the halls and the memories to visit a friend who had just given birth to her long-awaited daughter. I masked my tears and shared her joy...dancing the dance.

JC Penney sends me a Happy Birthday card announcing their photography studio specials for "LYDIA WHO'S ONE!" I'm surprised when I open the card, surprised that I didn't expect it, and surprised at my irrational hostility. I never want to buy anything at JC Penney again. Dancing the dance.

I sob like a baby, watching happy TV shows: sappy commercials, bad made-for-TV movies, Kathie Lee Gifford's stories about her kids. Life is so precious, and I'm grateful for each day that I have to share it with those that I love. Dancing the dance.

The dance of Lydia's life was painful because it ended much too soon. The dance of grief is one we're forced into, catching us off guard and sweeping us into its wretched rhythm. But if we're willing, God will join us there and comfort us. I find myself thinking about how different life would be if Lydia had never been here. "I could have missed the pain, but I'd have had to miss the dance."

Begin playing "The Dance." Pause or lower the music in the middle of the song so the audience can hear the speaker or worship leader read the following paraphrase of a passage from The Message.

"I will lift you up, God, because you lifted me out of the depths. There was a time when I screamed, 'Good Lord, where are you?' Then you touched my despairing soul with healing and delivered me from my own private hell. All who believe, give your praise to God. The nights of crying your eyes out give way to days of laughter. When things were going great, I felt secure. You favored me, Lord. Then you looked the other way, and I fell to pieces. I called out to you, Lord, holding on to hope by my fingernails. I cried for mercy. If I'm dead and gone, how can I praise you? Hear me and be merciful to me. Help me. Help me to dance. Change my wailing into whirling dance. Remove my clothing of despair and replace it with a cloak of joy. Lord, I'm about to burst with song; I can't keep quiet about you. God, my God, I love you so much. I'll dance anyway."

Finish playing "The Dance." Then have the worship leader lead the congregation in prayers for children or others. Have the band play "I Hope You Dance."

Provide words on-screen or in print for the following responsive closing.

LEADER: With the living and eternal God as our goal and guide, fear and anxiety need have no place in our lives.

ALL: So we choose to dance anyway.

LEADER: All the evil in the world cannot destroy the Lord, nor can it destroy anyone within God's loving embrace.

ALL: So we choose to dance anyway.

LEADER: We stand tall, regardless of threatening enemies and the pain of evil.

ALL: So we choose to dance anyway.

LEADER: Our God hears when we cry out and will not ignore our needs.

We dedicate ourselves anew to you, O Lord. We will serve you whatever the cost or the consequence. We will praise your name and proclaim your love to people all around.

Band leads congregation in songs of hope and celebration. Worship leader closes the service. Band reprises "We Danced Anyway" or other exit music.

Journey to the Cross

Word: Various excerpts from the gospels

Theme: Journey to the Cross

Felt Need: We all face fearful challenges, but God's resurrection power will ultimately prevail.

Desired Outcome: Participants will identify with Jesus and truly experience the journey to the cross.

Look: Palm branches with a cross in the distance

Throughout the celebration, Gospel readings will be interspersed with drama pieces and excerpts from Max Lucado's retelling of Jesus' challenging journey to the cross. Page numbers are noted for all story excerpts, taken from Max Lucado's book *And the Angels Were Silent* (Sisters, OR: Multnomah Books, 1992).

journey to the cross

In addition to your regular worship personnel, you'll need a guitarist, four readers (they could be vocalists from the worship team), five drama players, and a painter. The drama players should include three adults (two men and a woman), a teenage girl, and a child. The painter needs to have a large black canvas (approximately 6x6-foot), brushes, and white and red paint.

Opening Song: "Creed" (Rich Mullins)

Opening Words of Story: *And the Angels Were Silent*, page 22.

CALL TO WORSHIP

"We are going to Jerusalem," he told his disciples. "The Son of Man will be turned over to the leading priests and the teachers of the law, and they will say that he must die. They will give the Son of Man to the…people to laugh at him and beat him with whips and crucify him. But on the third day, he will be raised to life again" (Matthew 20:18-19, *New Century Version*).

The New Testament gospel of Matthew details this account: "As they approached Jerusalem and came to Bethphage on the Mount of Olives, Jesus sent two disciples, saying to them, 'Go to the village ahead of you, and at once you will find a donkey tied there, with her colt by her. Untie them and bring them to me. If anyone says anything to you, tell him that the Lord needs them, and he will send them right away.' [Matthew 21:1-3]

"The disciples went and did as Jesus had instructed them. They brought the donkey and the colt, placed their cloaks on them, and Jesus sat on them. A very large crowd spread their cloaks on the road, while others cut branches from the trees and spread them on the road. The crowds that went ahead of him and those that followed shouted, 'Hosanna to the Son of David! Blessed is he who comes in the name of the Lord. Hosanna in the highest!'

"When Jesus entered Jerusalem, the whole city was stirred and asked, 'Who is this?' The crowds answered, 'This is Jesus, the prophet from Nazareth in Galilee.' " [Matthew 21:6-11]

VOCALIST 1: This is the One who was born to die.

VOCALIST 2: This is the One who shows us the way.

VOCALIST 3: This is the One who heals our diseases, who bears our grief, and carries our sorrow.

VOCALIST 4: This is the One we have grown to love...

WORSHIP LEADER: The Ancient of Days...let's stand and worship together!

SONG CELEBRATION

"Ancient of Days" (Jamie Harvell and Gary Sadler)
"Glory to Glory to Glory" (Fred Hammond)
"Here I Am to Worship" (Tim Hughes)

WORSHIP LEADER: We want to continue giving our best worship to the One who gave so much for us. In a moment we are asking the ushers to come for the offerings we've brought to share. First, hear these next words from Jesus' journey:

Days later while in Jerusalem, one of the teachers of the law came to Jesus and asked him, "Of all the commandments, which is the most important?" "The most important one is this," answered Jesus. "Love the Lord your God with all your heart, soul, mind, and strength."

"Well said, teacher," the man replied. "I believe you are right in saying that we should love God this way. It is more important than all burnt offerings and sacrifices."

When Jesus saw that the man understood, he said to him, "You are not far from the kingdom of God." [adapted from Mark 12:28-34]

Let's worship by giving our offerings now.

Have the band play as the offering is collected.

STORY OF MARY ANOINTING JESUS
And the Angels Were Silent, pages 48-50.

As the story is read, have drama players silently act out the roles of Jesus and Mary.

WORSHIP LEADER: That week, Jesus was in the home of a man known as Simon the leper, a man Jesus had healed. And while he was there, one woman's act of worship was so expensive, so extravagant, it seized the moment entirely…

Song (sung by dramatic Mary or another vocalist)*:* "Alabaster Box" (CeCe Winans)

Story: Read the account of the Last Supper from *The Message* (Matthew 26:17-37). End the reading just before Jesus' prayer in Gethsemane. As the story is read, display numerous classic art depictions of the Last Supper on-screen.

DRAMATIC JESUS: Father, oh my Father. Everything is possible with you. I've seen it over and over again. It was you who calmed the sea when they were so afraid. You who brought Lazarus back to life after he'd been gone three days. You parted the Red Sea with your mighty hand. Father, you made a way when they were so afraid. Everything is possible with you. And now, I am the one afraid. I do not want to die the death that is coming…except that they need me so much. They *need* a Savior. They are broken, Father. But if it will heal them, if it will make a way for them to be with us, I will go, Father. I'd do anything for them. *(Pause.)* Not my will, but yours be done. *(Jesus bows his head and the lights go down.)*

As the band plays "Love Song" (Third Day), have the drama players and the painter perform the drama described below.

"Jesus" gets up from his Gethsemane prayer as the guitarist begins playing and singing the song. Jesus walks over to the painter (dressed all in black) and touches her hands, "commissioning her" to begin painting. She turns to her large black canvas and begins painting a crude Jesus figure on the cross with white paint.

Jesus turns to the first drama scene, a husband and wife bitterly fighting as a young child looks on. The two adults turn away from each other. Jesus reaches down and hugs the child, hugs the mother, and attempts to hug the dad, who is angry and refuses. Jesus, very concerned, then joins mother with child and "blesses" them with a hug. The family freezes in place.

Next Jesus goes to a scene where a younger man is talking animatedly on a cell phone. As Jesus comes near, the man apparently receives some very bad news on the phone and slumps down, devastated. Jesus attempts to comfort this man, who is visibly shaken and crying. Seeing that Jesus cares, the man pulls out his wallet and shows him pictures of his family, indicating that the bad news must have been in regard to someone very close. Jesus hugs him and assures him of his presence and care. The man freezes in place.

As Jesus gets up, he is drawn to a third scene, a teenage girl who is obsessing over her weight (in an imaginary mirror) and then vomits into an imaginary toilet. Jesus pauses and is so taken in by this that he walks to her, lifts up her chin, and in sign language says, "You are beautiful to me." The girl smiles faintly and they touch both hands so as to say that Jesus will be staying in her life. The girl freezes in place.

Jesus slowly turns around to take one last look at each of the drama scenes, then turns and heads back to the painter's canvas. By now the painter has finished the crude "Jesus on the cross" painting with white on black, and has added touches of bright red paint as indication of the blood, pain, and suffering. Jesus steps up on a small stool in front of the canvas and aligns his arms and body with the painted figure, dropping his head as though dying.

One by one, each of the drama players (with the exception of the angry husband, who is still turned away) turns and extends both arms toward Jesus, ending with the painter herself doing the same. Behind all of this, we hear the refrain of the love song: "Just to be with you, I'd do anything…"

Slow lighting transition and soft piano music guide the transition toward the following questions (excerpted from And the Angels Were Silent, *page 25) delivered by the worship leader.*

WORSHIP LEADER: Is there a Jerusalem on your horizon? Are you carrying a heavy cross?

Closing Song: "No Weapon" (Fred Hammond)

(Appropriate closing words of your choosing.)

Armor of God

Set: Set up a "fashion runway" in your worship area. Small white Christmas lights work well to mark off the runway.

Actors/Costumes: You'll need a fashion show host and six models. Models should wear clothing similar to the clothing described below, including items that represent the belt of truth, breastplate of righteousness, feet (shoes) fitted with readiness, shield of faith, helmet of salvation, and sword of the Spirit. (We found most of our "armor" at a party costume shop.)

FASHION SHOW HOST: Good evening (morning), ladies and gentlemen. And who wouldn't want to be a sharp dressed man or woman? And so tonight (today), we present to you a magnificent fashion event to challenge the current state of the closet and to consider all-new and improved options for weekend worshippers' wardrobes. Put on these latest accessories, and you're sure to be "dressed for success."

Our first model is Sean, a summer media intern, all dressed up and no place to go! But Sean's tux is no everyday black tie number. Sean is featuring the *belt of truth*, representing a rock-solid worldview. With this belt in place, the truth about God's purposes in the world becomes amazingly clear. Available in women's sizes as well.

Christopher of Dayton, Ohio, is just in off his Harley, and a fashion statement to behold. Chris sports for us the *breastplate of righteousness*, a must-have for anyone susceptible to the wind, rain, sleet, and guilt—yes, guilt. For this breastplate carries the declaration that what righteousness we have is in God alone. (Chris makes it easy to believe that!) So if you're out riding and feeling some remorse or need of forgiveness, be sure to nab your own. Comes in silver, gold, or silver and gold.

Now, have you felt a little apprehensive about life? Fearful to take your next steps of faith? Check out these gospel galoshes, *feet fitted with readiness* of the gospel. Our summer worship intern, Sarah, says they feel oh-so-nice and now looks forward to wherever God takes her, although most days Sarah says, "There's no place like home." *(Model clicks heels three times.)* Try these on for size when the future looks bleak and your steps get stuck.

We all know that "stuff happens"—it happens to everyone. But what about when bad things happen to good people? They pull out the *shield of faith*, guaranteed to ward off stray arrows, harsh criticisms, and the general barrage of day-to-day digs. Erica, recent UD graduate, claims that all people of faith need a shield of their own. Mahvelous, dahling!

A day on the beach can be hard on the hair. What to do to tame those tresses? Matthew, media associate at Ginghamsburg, shares the secret of his success: the *helmet of salvation*. This headwear not only covers a multitude of bad hair days, but also provides a sense of security about just where you stand with God. Just ask Matt. Beach towel and flip flops sold separately.

Lastly, we feature the *sword of the Spirit*, a slick stick wielding wondrous power, wonder-working power from the Word of God. Heidi of Tipp City wants you to know that swords are not just for guys anymore. It's all a matter of putting it to use. The power is in the Word—the Word of God. Watch it work for you.

And that's it, ladies and gentlemen. We hope you've been inspired to acquire your own armor of God so you, too, can be dressed for success! Back to you, (Francie)...

WORSHIP LEADER: Without the armor of God, we don't have what it takes to fight the good fight. We come today to be challenged to put on whatever it takes to honor Jesus, our Lord and King.

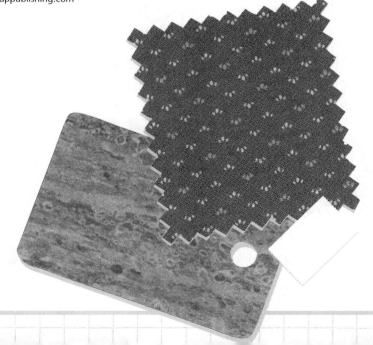

Sample Scripts for Worship Celebrations

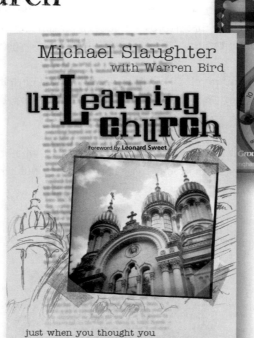